CW00523830

DEAR BIBLE,
I have a
PROBLEM

DEAR BIBLE,
I have a
PROBLEM

Mike Coles shares some 'agony aunt'
letters to the Bible... **and the replies!**

Published by
The Bible Reading Fellowship
First Floor, Elsfield Hall
15–17 Elsfield Way, Oxford OX2 8FG
Website: www.brf.org.uk

ISBN 1 84101 368 4
First published 2005
10 9 8 7 6 5 4 3 2 1 0

Acknowledgments
Unless otherwise stated, scripture quotations are taken from the Good News
Bible published by The Bible Societies/HarperCollins Publishers Ltd, UK
© American Bible Society 1966, 1971, 1976, 1992, used with permission.

Scripture quotations taken from the *Holy Bible, New International Version*,
copyright © 1973, 1978, 1984 by International Bible Society. Used by
permission of Hodder & Stoughton Limited. All rights reserved. 'NIV' is a
registered trademark of International Bible Society. UK trademark number
1448790.

Scripture quotations taken from The Revised Standard Version of the Bible,
copyright © 1946, 1952, 1971 by the Division of Christian Education of the
National Council of the Churches of Christ in the United States of America,
are used by permission. All rights reserved.

A catalogue record for this book is available from the British Library

Printed in Singapore by Craft Print International Ltd

Introduction

Listen up, folks! The Bible isn't just any old book. It's the Number One Book! It is the most powerful way in which God speaks to us.

Psalm 119:105 says, 'Your word is a lamp to guide me and a light for my path.' The Bible is my light and guide. When I read the Bible, God's word, it gives me strength and renews my spirit.

Did you know that the Bible is the world's best-selling book? And that it relates to every area of our lives? There's so much in it. You name it, it's there: all types of adventure and romance. It deals with every kind of sin from murder and rape to lying and adultery. We read about people who are troubled, depressed or lonely, victims of bullying and all kinds of family problems. Everyday problems are also dealt with in the Bible, because the Bible is for everyday people; it really can help us in our daily lives, with all the problems that life throws at us. In this book I will give plenty of examples of how the Bible can help and advise us when things aren't going so well.

Many people, especially younger teenagers, love to read problem pages in newspapers and magazines, so I thought I would write this book in the style of a problem page. In this case the 'agony aunt' is the Bible, and I have written letters from a range of imaginary people, asking the Bible about some of the many problems that we face day by day. In reply, I have written as the 'agony aunt Bible', showing how God's word can respond with real advice and help. Many of the examples I use will focus on teenagers and the many problems they face as they grow up. Having taught in a secondary school for more than 18 years, and also worked as a tutor and counsellor, I've certainly heard a few of these.

Just to show how the Bible has an answer or a piece of great advice to any problem you may have, try these for starters. To those people who sadly say, 'No one really loves me', it's wonderful to be able to turn to John 3:16 and tell them that God loves them. When kids at school get into a state and say that something is impossible,

I tell them, 'Well, not according to the Bible, which tells us that all things are possible for God' (Luke 18:27).

Before we start with the first 'Dear Bible' letter, here is a 'recipe' that one of my pupils brought into school for me. The author is unknown, but I think it's excellent! It's great to have it here in the beginning of the book, because God's word really can work miracles in your life.

Recipe for a miracle
1 cup of tension
2 cups of stress
$1^1/_2$ teaspoons of guilt
2 heaped cups of limited time
$^3/_4$ tablespoon of urgency
A dash of 'no other choice'
3 heaped cups of faith
Unlimited love

1. Fold ingredients gently into a bowl. Mix vigorously and add a few tears.
2. You'll sweat a little as you knead the dough. Pack it firmly between your hopes and dreams and form into a perfect little ball.
3. Sprinkle it with a little faith (we recommend Hebrews 11), rolling the ball in the faith until fully covered.
4. Place it under a veil of belief and allow it to rise.
5. Put it in an oven that has been pre-set at the perfect temperature for the heat of trials and tribulations.
6. Allow it to brown under the warmth of God's love. Remove after due season and allow to cool in the confidence of his promise.
7. Garnish with your praises. Arrange neatly on a platter of thankfulness and serve to friends, families and, oh yes, strangers... invite them too!
8. Pass on the recipe to all who request it and let them know that with this recipe, they have the makings of a miracle!

Letter 1

Dear Bible, I have a problem. My name is Rachel and I am 15 years old. I have recently moved to a new town with my parents. We have lived here for a few months now, and my problem is that I am finding it very difficult to make any friends. I speak to people at school and at church on Sundays, but that's as far as it ever goes. I don't have anyone I can really call my friend. I pray about it, but I really would like some advice from you. How can I make some good friends? Please help me. Thank you, Rachel.

Dear Rachel, first of all, I thank you very much for writing to me. I was sorry to hear that you're having a problem with making friends in your new town. I hope that the advice I give you will help you sort out this problem.

Before we look at some practical advice for you, Rachel, I'm sure I don't need to remind you of the one true friend you already have: Jesus! Jesus loves you so much that he died for you on the cross. He gave his life for you. Reflect on this passage, Rachel: *The greatest love a person can have for his friends is to give his life for them.*[1]

You say that you have been praying regularly about your problem. Well, that's good, as it means that Jesus, your greatest friend, will have heard your prayers, and as you follow my advice he will be with you all the way.

The most important bit of advice I'm going to give you is this: be friendly! People are always attracted to those who are friendly and don't appear to be a threat. As well as being friendly, do show a real interest in those you speak to, and some of them may end up as good friends.

Obviously you can't be good friends with everyone who is friendly to you. All people have different personalities, interests, upbringing, likes and dislikes. Some people would drive you mad if they were close friends of yours. Here's what you could try to find some likely friends.

Out of all the people your age whom you know at the moment, whether at school or at church, think of someone who seems to share similar interests to you. Obviously, as a Christian, you may wish to find another Christian friend your age. Let's see if we can now turn such a person into a friend.

You'll need to start by having a brief chat with this person next time you see them. People of your age often like to chat about music, fashion, TV, hobbies, what you get up to after school and at weekends. Find out what this person really likes. If it sounds interesting, maybe you could find out more, so that you can talk further if and when you meet them again.

If you feel that you are far too nervous to talk, try again another time when you feel more confident. If you feel you'll never be confident, then you could talk to someone at church about this, or your parents or teacher, or somebody else you trust.

If your chat goes quite well with this potential friend, try inviting them along to a youth group, sports or music event. It's always good to meet again in a group, with other people around, before inviting your new friend straight to your house or some other 'one-to-one' situation, in case you both find it difficult to talk about anything and it gets a little awkward.

Rachel, if things don't work out the first or second time, please remember that there are other people around who will prove to be good friends for you. Just keep trying, enjoy the trying—and, above all, stay friendly.

I hope that very soon you will discover that true friendship is one of the greatest gifts of life. *'Two are better off than one,'* wrote a wise man in one of my books.[2] When you find some true friends, Rachel, as I know you will soon, remember this: genuine friends must be cherished and never forsaken. As Proverbs says, *'Do not forget your friends.'*[3]

I wish you all the best in the future, and I know that soon you'll have made some very good friends. If you would ever like to write to me again for any advice, I would love to hear from you.

The Bible

Letter 2

Dear Bible, I have a problem. My name is Becky and I'm 21 years old. I think I have found the man I want to marry! I think it's true love. The only thing on my mind at the moment, though, is 'what is true love?' I really do need to know if I truly love this man, and whether he is the one I'm going to marry. Could you help me?

✤

My dear Becky, I was very excited to hear that you might have found your 'true love'. It must be a wonderful feeling for you. It was wise of you to write to me, for although it is probably a very exciting time for you, it is also a time when you are facing one of the most important decisions you will ever make: 'Is this the man I want to spend the rest of my life with?' You are correct, therefore, in asking yourself, 'Have I found the right one? Is this true love?'

Well, Becky, there is a passage in one of my books that immediately springs to mind and may well help you to answer your question. It is probably my most well-known passage regarding love: Paul's first letter to the Corinthians, chapter 13. Here are a few verses, which I think you will find most helpful.

Love is patient and kind; it is not jealous or conceited or proud; love is not ill-mannered or selfish or irritable; love does not keep a record of wrongs; love is not happy with evil, but is happy with the truth. Love never gives up; and its faith, hope, and patience never fail.' [4]

Quite simply, Becky, this is what love is all about. You want to know what true love is? Well, a truly loving relationship needs to contain these qualities. My New Testament is all about a man who was full of every one of these qualities: Jesus Christ. If what you have found in your relationship is a sense of patience and kindness, and there is no element of selfishness, then you may well have found your 'true love'.

There are people who seem to look for other qualities instead, such as good looks, or a fast car or large house. I'm sure this doesn't apply to you, Becky, but it is sad how many people look for these qualities. If they do, their relationship is almost certainly heading for disaster. Another verse that links in here is when God says to Samuel, '*I do not judge as people judge. They look at the outward appearance, but I look at the heart.*'[5]

I do hope that I have been of some help to you, Becky. I have told you what qualities make up 'real' love, and from what I have told you, from what you sense in your heart and through prayer, I'm sure you will be able to answer your question about whether or not you have found true love.

By the way, if, in time, you do go on to marry, enjoy that wonderful book contained in my Old Testament: the Song of Songs. You'll love it, as it's a real celebration of love and sex between a man and a woman.

With love,

The Bible

Letter 3

Dear Bible, my name is Samantha and I'm 17 years old. The reason I'm writing is that I feel lonely and I sometimes feel that I have no control over my life. My parents are divorced and I have recently moved to a new town with my mum. I have been unable to settle down or feel at home, and I'm feeling more and more under pressure. I started eating to comfort myself and then instantly felt guilty about it. As if it were the natural thing to do, I made myself sick. Ever since then, I have been doing this several times a day. This is one area of my life where I feel that I am in control. My mother has discovered that there is something going on with my eating habits, and she's constantly questioning me about it. How can I make her realize that for once I am in control and know what I'm doing, unlike in all the other areas of my life?

Dear Samantha, I am very sorry to hear that you are hurting at the moment, and I hope that by sharing with you some of my teachings, I might be able to help you.

You mention a few different issues in your letter. You write that your parents are divorced, and that you feel lonely—quite possibly because you've recently moved to a new town with your mum and don't know anybody. You mention that you feel as if you have no control in your life at the moment, given your circumstances. These are obviously all very important issues, and you may find some help with your loneliness from my answers to some of the letters I've written to other people here.

What really concerns me, Samantha, is the issue of your eating and making yourself sick, and then feeling that this puts you in control. It's only right to say that I believe you have a very dangerous eating disorder called bulimia. You may not believe this, but maybe as many as one out of every six young women will have some sort of eating disorder before they are in their mid-20s.

If you are suffering from bulimia, I urge you to get medical help as soon as possible, as it is a complex illness, affecting you both physically and mentally. Your doctor can advise on the best way of treating the condition.

Seeing as you wrote to me, the Bible, though, I assume that it's more than practical help that you want. Let's look at a few spiritual issues.

The first truth I would like to share with you, Samantha, is how valuable you are to God. He loves you so much, and you have been created in his image. Even a tiny sparrow has value in God's eyes, so how much more valuable are you to him?[6] Your body itself is very precious: it actually belongs to God.

Don't you know that your body is the temple of the Holy Spirit, who lives in you and who was given to you by God? You do not belong to yourselves but to God.[7]

When you start receiving some medical help, Samantha, I hope it will not be too long before you begin to understand that this really isn't the way to treat your body. Eating and then making yourself sick all the time will slowly wear you down, and you could destroy that most wonderful creation, your body. Elsewhere in my book are teachings on the wonder of life before birth, how the body is beautifully formed inside the mother's womb.

You created every part of me... When my bones were being formed, carefully put together in my mother's womb, when I was growing there in secret, you knew that I was there—you saw me before I was born.[8]

I know that in your letter you wrote about feeling 'in control'. I guess that, to you, life seems pretty out of control, with your parents' divorce, feeling lonely and moving house. Taking control of what you are eating is your way of coping with everything. It needs to be said, though, that this eating habit of yours is probably controlling you.

Do you feel guilty about your parents' divorce in some way? Perhaps you're scared of what the future holds for you? Whatever the reason, you have chosen to punish yourself. All my teachings point to one thing, Samantha, which is that God really wants to work in your life and give you peace. Please let him take control of things. Turn to God: *'leave your troubles with the Lord'*.[9] Whatever your worries and problems, just *'leave all your worries with him, because he cares for you'*.[10]

There are no easy answers to give you, Samantha. I beg you to seek medical help. Turn to God; pour out your heart to him, and he will truly comfort you. When Hannah prayed, in 1 Samuel 1, because she was so sad about not being able to have a child, she wept bitterly and poured her heart out to God. That's the way to pray; don't hide anything.

God loves you so much. Let him take control of your life and— God bless you, Samantha.

The Bible

Letter 4

Dear Bible, I have a problem. My name is David and I'm 23 years old. The problem is basically this. I think I am really ugly. My time at school was awful, because I was always being teased about my looks. I've never really had many friends. I've never had a girlfriend, and that's probably because I'm so ugly. Why have I been made like this? Why do I look so ugly? This problem is taking over my life and I feel so down about it. Could you please help me?

Dear David, I am sorry to hear that you had such an awful time at school, and I'm sorry to hear that you feel so down because you believe that you're ugly!

I'm afraid I'm going to have to begin by saying that if you think you are ugly, then you are also saying that God is ugly! In Genesis it says, *'So God created human beings, making them to be like himself.'* [11]

My dear David, this passage clearly teaches that you were made in God's image. This is a wonderful thing, a beautiful thing. There should be no talk of anyone being ugly. Sadly, there are many in your society who judge people by the way they look. There are thousands of magazines with so-called 'gorgeous' women and 'handsome' men, but anybody who has ever teased you about your looks and called you ugly is living a pretty shallow life. All that's important to them is how someone looks; and anyway, how dare they decide who is 'good looking' and who is 'ugly'?

I know a wonderful passage, David, that makes this point very clearly indeed. It's the story of Samuel, he is looking for the next king of Israel to replace Saul. Samuel travels to Bethlehem to visit Jesse, as it is one of Jesse's sons who is to be the next king. When he arrives, he sees the first of the sons, called Eliab, and he is so impressed by Eliab's looks that he assumes this is the man that God will choose as the next king. But God says to Samuel:

Pay no attention to how tall and handsome he is. I have rejected him, because I do not judge as people judge. They look at the outward appearance, but I look at the heart.[12]

You see, David, this is what's most important. There are those who simply judge others by how they look. Sadly, you've encountered people like that, and it has brought you quite low. This is understandable, because people can be cruel, and words do hurt. But there are those who see beyond mere looks. There will be many who will see you for what you are—a unique child of God—and that, David, is special and beautiful.

Let me share with you another amazing fact. When God sent his only son Jesus into the world, you would have thought that he'd be something pretty special to look at. This was God's only son, for goodness' sake! David, you may think you are ugly. Well, read this, and see how Jesus was described by a prophet speaking many years before he was even born:

He had no dignity or beauty to make us take notice of him. There was nothing attractive about him, nothing that would draw us to him. We despised him and rejected him; he endured suffering and pain. No one would even look at him—we ignored him as if he were nothing.[13]

You don't get a much more 'ugly' description of someone than that. But despite his appearance, just look at what this man Jesus Christ did. God had a wonderful plan for him to save humanity, and, David, God also has a wonderful plan for you. Through prayer and regular reading of the lessons and stories that I hold, you will find out what his plan is for you. You stick with God; let him get to work in your life. When this starts to happen, people will see what a beautiful person you are. You'll make real friends, people who see your heart, not your outward appearance.

You're a child of God, David, made in his image. I hope I have been able to comfort you in some way and that you feel strengthened to go out into the world and make a difference. Let people see you for who you really are.

God bless you, David.

The Bible

Letter 5

Dear Bible, I have a problem. My name is Sharon, and I'm 17 years old. I feel so, so lonely. I have good parents who love me, but there is no one else in life that I can relate to or spend time with. I attend a Sixth Form College, but don't really hang around with anyone there. I feel awful, so alone. It's the worst feeling in the world. Is there something wrong with me? I feel I'm a good person, I attend church and pray to God, and yet I'm alone. Could you please give me some advice? I don't feel I can cope with this awful loneliness any more.

My dear Sharon, how awful it was to read your letter. I could sense the pain you are feeling and the utter despair. I have heard people describe loneliness as one of the most universal sources of human suffering, and I know it must be affecting you both emotionally and physically.

People have different way of expressing what it means for them to be lonely. Perhaps, Sharon, you feel painfully aware that you lack any meaningful contact with other people. Maybe you feel totally empty inside. Lonely people often describe themselves as being extremely sad, isolated, discouraged. Whatever is behind this awful feeling of loneliness you are experiencing, Sharon, I promise you that contained within me, the Bible, will be the advice and comfort you need.

As a Christian, Sharon, I think it's important for you to realize the awful times of loneliness faced by many of the well-known characters of which I tell, throughout their lives. Imagine poor Mary, at such a young age, being told that she was to have a child without being married. Who on earth was going to believe such a story? She must have felt very lonely and isolated. What about many of the Old Testament prophets, like Jeremiah? How lonely must they have felt throughout their lives!

Moses must have had many lonely moments and episodes of despair when leading that complaining bunch of people out of Egypt. And then there's the story of Joseph and his brothers. The brothers actually wanted to kill him! He was sold as a slave, accused of rape and thrown into prison. If anyone won prizes for loneliness, I'm sure Joseph would receive a few.

When Jesus faced his darkest hour in the garden of Gethsemane, he said, *'The sorrow in my heart is so great that it almost crushes me.'* [14] He had asked his three closest disciples, Peter, James and John, to accompany him. But they fell asleep in Jesus' greatest hour of need. The feelings of loneliness and despair he must have felt at that moment are unimaginable.

So you can see, Sharon, that I hold many examples of people experiencing the most awful situations. Remember that you are not alone; that is the starting point for the way I'm going to help you and give you the advice that you requested in your letter.

All these Bible characters experienced loneliness and yet they were able to deal with it during their lives. Jesus experienced loneliness. He *knows* what you are feeling, Sharon. Isn't that wonderful? He truly knows the pain you have in your heart, and he can comfort you. He has promised to be with you, to stay by your side: *'And I will be with you always, to the end of the age.'* [15]

You told me, Sharon, that you attend church and pray regularly. Well, I want you to remember this promise of Jesus to be with you. He is with you now, feeling the pain that you are going through.

Let's see what other help I can offer you to deal with your situation. Paul the apostle must have felt very lonely at times, almost at the point of despair. How did he deal with this problem? Well, in his second letter to Timothy he writes, *'But the Lord stayed with me and gave me strength.'* [16]

He was helped by being truly aware of God's presence in his life. Are you aware of him in your life, Sharon? Just as that was a comfort to Paul, so it could also be for you. When you have this amazing sense of God's presence with you, it can give you great hope and strength. When Jesus poured out his heart in the garden of Gethsemane in that moment of awful loneliness, we read that *'an angel from heaven appeared to him and strengthened him'.*[17]

Jesus endured what you're going through now, Sharon; and just as he was strengthened, he will strengthen you now. Here are some of his own words, which I hope will comfort and strengthen you. *'When I go, you will not be left all alone; I will come back to you.'*[18] And also, *'"Do not be worried and upset," Jesus told them. "Believe in God and believe also in me."'*[19]

Another passage that may comfort you, Sharon, is from the book of Isaiah: *'Do not be afraid—I am with you! I am your God—let nothing terrify you! I will make you strong and help you; I will protect you and save you.'*[20]

I'm sure there have been many moments in your life when your loneliness has been almost terrifying, but with my help we are going to conquer it. That awful, empty place that you feel inside you is going to be filled with the healing and powerful love of God, who will comfort, protect and save you. As written in one of my Psalms, *'He heals the broken-hearted and bandages their wounds.'*[21]

There are many more beautiful passages contained within me, which I know will help you so much. You will discover them in time, and of course, should you ever write back to me, I will be happy to share further teachings with you.

I would guess, Sharon, that you might be after a little practical help as well. Here are a few ideas for you to try.

Sometimes people have problems with their communication skills, and this can really contribute to loneliness. If you are not sure how to talk or relate to others, this will often stop people from relating or wanting to chat to you. If you feel that this might apply to you, then don't worry. Problems like this can easily be sorted out. You may want to chat to your parents about it first, or maybe your church minister. I know you attend a Sixth Form College, Sharon. At all such places of learning, there is always someone who is responsible for student counselling. There may even be a teacher you really trust and get on well with. They will always listen and help to point you in the right direction. Perhaps they might suggest some classes or counselling that you could attend to improve your communication and relational skills. Rest assured, Sharon, there is definitely help out there that could sort out this problem—if, indeed, you think it could be part of the reason why you are feeling so lonely.

By being strengthened and comforted by the words contained within me, I hope you will start to think more positively. Positive thinking will always help in defeating loneliness.

I'm not sure if you have hobbies. If you don't, consider getting involved with something you think you might enjoy. Try something new. Keep busy.

Actually, Sharon, speaking about trying something new, I'm sure God has blessed you with some spiritual gifts. Perhaps there is some way you can help in the body of Christ, the church family. Getting more involved in your church would be great for you. You'd meet others, be encouraged to share your faith, and have fun. You can read about spiritual gifts and working as part of the body of Christ in Paul's letter to the Romans, chapter 12.

I hope I have been of some help to you, Sharon. I'm so glad you wrote to me. This loneliness won't go away by itself, but I hope that I have been able to point you in the right direction. Remember, you are never alone. God is always with you, and you can draw close to him in prayer and by reflecting on the wonderful words contained within me.

God bless you, Sharon.

The Bible

Letter 6

Dear Bible, I have a problem. I have recently become a Christian and accepted Jesus Christ as my Saviour, which is great. The problem, though, is this. I come from a Jewish family. My family is a good family and I love them dearly, but my conversion to Christianity is causing a problem. They constantly question me about why I have done it. And it's not just my parents who are involved. My grandparents, uncles and aunts are concerned as well. I worry that the situation is just going to get worse and worse, so I urgently need some advice on how to deal with it.

My dear friend—I'll call you 'friend' as you didn't leave me your name—thank you so much for taking the time to write to me and sharing your problem. I have to say how delighted I was to hear that you have accepted Jesus Christ as your saviour. I'm also looking forward to sharing with you how this should not be a huge problem for you and your family. I was glad to read in your letter that you have a good family and that you love them dearly. That is certainly a good starting point, as is the fact that you are all believers in the One God.

What immediately sprang to mind when I read your letter, dear friend, is the account about Nicodemus in John's Gospel, chapter 3, verses 1 to 22. This man was a Pharisee, and yet he came to realize that Jesus was indeed the Messiah. Jesus even spoke to Nicodemus about being born again. It is interesting to ponder how Nicodemus got along with his family after telling them that he believed Jesus was the Son of God. Did they reject him? I'm sure he would have faced some problems.

Whatever happened, we read later in John's Gospel how Nicodemus continued to support Jesus. When Jesus appeared on trial before the unbelieving Jewish authorities, it was Nicodemus who spoke up for him, saying, '*According to our Law we cannot condemn anyone before hearing him and finding out what he has done.*'[22]

We can also read in John's Gospel that Nicodemus was there at the end to anoint the body of Jesus: '*Nicodemus, who at first had gone to see Jesus at night, went with Joseph, taking with him about 30 kilogrammes of spices, a mixture of myrrh and aloes.*'[23]

So you see, my dear friend, even way back then, there was someone in a fairly similar situation to yours: a Jew who had accepted Jesus as the Messiah. And think about Jesus' disciples. They accepted that Jesus was the Messiah, and many of them would have had to explain this to their families.

One thing that I would suggest you do is to try and find people who are in a similar position to yours. There is an organization called 'Jews for Jesus'. As Jews, they believe that Jesus is the Messiah. If you can locate your nearest group, you may well find them a great help.

Now I would like to share some facts with you, my dear friend, which I hope can smooth things over with you and your extended family. Remember, first of all, that Jesus himself was a Jew. He worshipped in the synagogue and the temple. He celebrated all the Jewish festivals.

Remember also that Christians believe in the Old Testament, which you would previously have called your Jewish Scripture. Although you now accept Jesus as Messiah, this does not mean that you have to reject all your Jewish customs and the Old Testament. Let your family know this. Tell them that you're proud of your Jewish heritage. I would advise you to continue taking part in all the Jewish celebrations, observing the Sabbath, Passover and so on. At the same time you can start attending church on a Sunday, do regular Bible study including the New Testament, and pray regularly to Jesus. Your family will probably struggle to adjust to these changes, but if you keep observing the Jewish practices as well, this should help to smooth out the difficulties.

Your family may question you about reading the New Testament. You can point out to them that in no way is the New Testament anti-Jewish. Nearly all the New Testament writers worshipped regularly in the synagogue and the temple. They certainly all knew their Jewish Scripture. Paul, who wrote 13 of the New Testament books, was a descendant of Abraham, a member of the tribe of Benjamin. He was also a learned Pharisee, and his amazing knowledge and understanding of the Jewish tradition always played an important part in his preaching.

It is this 'Jewishness' that you should be emphasizing when you discuss these issues with your family. There is a huge link between Christians and Jews because of the importance of the Old Testament. Try to work on what you have in common, especially your belief in the One God, creator of the universe.

The major difference that you and your family will face when reading the Jewish Scripture (or the Old Testament) together is that, as far as you are concerned, the New Testament that you will also now be reading is the fulfilment of the Old.

The Gospels make numerous references to the Jewish Scripture, demonstrating how Old Testament prophecy is fulfilled in Jesus. For example, his conception was prophesied in Isaiah 7:14, and Matthew, in his Gospel, writes, *'Now all this happened in order to make what the Lord had said through the prophet come true, "A virgin will become pregnant and have a son, and he will be called Immanuel" (which means, "God is with us").'*[24]

Matthew also quotes an Old Testament prophet to demonstrate that his prophecy about the birthplace of the Messiah has been fulfilled: *'For this is what the prophet wrote: "Bethlehem in the land of Judah, you are by no means the least of the leading cities of Judah; for from you will come a leader who will guide my people Israel."'*[25]

My dear friend, I am making this point at length to remind you that although you and your family will continue to read Jewish Scriptures together, as far as you are now concerned, the Old Testament all points to Jesus. This may well be the major point of friction for you and your family.

But, as I said earlier, do hold on to your wonderful Jewish heritage. Attend the synagogue, observe Jewish practices, and continue to love and honour your parents and the rest of the family.

Work on all the ways in which you can still be united. When your parents or other family members want to discuss this issue with you, make sure you always remain calm and respectful. Make it clear that you have certainly not rejected them, and don't ever try to convince them that you are right and they are wrong.

Ultimately, my dear friend, you are still part of their family. You said that there was plenty of love present. Well, I'm sure that it will see you through. Let me remind you again: you all believe in the One God. Open your hearts to him in regular prayer. In time, maybe others will see the Jewish Scriptures in the way that you now see them, and remember, do try to contact others who are in a similar position to you.

Dear friend, thank you for writing to me, and I hope that you will find peace within your family, and that this problem will not get out of hand. I wish you all the best.

The Bible

Letter 7

Dear Bible, my name is Alan, and it's a good friend of mine who has a problem. She's asked me for some advice. I won't give her name, but I can tell you that she is a lovely person and a practising Christian. A couple of months ago, she went to a party and met a man. In a moment of weakness one thing led to another and they slept together. She felt really bad about this, and knew that she had sinned. However, the problem has now become a little more serious. She has discovered that she is pregnant. She is devastated and doesn't know where to turn or what to do. She has even been asking me whether she should keep the baby. I thought I would turn to God's word to get some advice. Please could you help me to help my friend? What should I tell her? I look forward to hearing from you.

Dear Alan, your friend is clearly very lucky to have someone like you by her side at this difficult time. I'm very sorry to hear that she is going through a tough patch at the moment, and it must be hard for you, seeing your friend suffer like this. I'm so pleased that you have written to me, and I hope that you may find some answers in what I say.

Before I suggest some practical advice, I'd like you to be able to tell her that God is with her at this difficult time. Psalm 46 is a wonderful place to start. Here are a few verses:

God is our shelter and strength, always ready to help in times of trouble. So we will not be afraid, even if the earth is shaken and mountains fall into the ocean depths; even if the seas roar and rage, and the hills are shaken by the violence… The Lord Almighty is with us; the God of Jacob is our refuge.[26]

The next point I'd like to address, Alan, is that your letter said your friend realized she had sinned and felt really bad. I would imagine that she is still feeling terrible. It wouldn't surprise me if she feels that she has committed the most awful sin and may never be forgiven.

This is a natural response when we have sinned, because God has blessed everyone with a conscience. It's like an inbuilt alarm system. When you are tempted to do something that goes against the word of God, your alarm bell sounds, and you should be guided to make the right decision. But, as Paul wrote in his letter to the Romans, *'All have sinned and fall short of the glory of God.'*[27]

Everybody sins, Alan. Every Christian, every day, has to fight against temptation. As Jesus said to his disciples in the garden of Gethsemane before his arrest, *'Keep watch and pray that you will not fall into temptation. The spirit is willing, but the flesh is weak.'*[28]

Your friend clearly has a good heart and conscience, and she knows that she has sinned. What she also needs to know is that her loving heavenly Father will forgive her sin. You must realize, Alan, that God may hate all sin, but he truly loves the sinner. Reassure your friend that she must no longer feel awful about having sinned. She knows in her heart that she made a mistake. God knows that too, and she can ask for and receive his forgiveness. To conclude this point, I'd like to share a few words from a psalmist.

Be merciful to me, O God, because of your constant love. Because of your great mercy wipe away my sins! Wash away all my evil and make me clean from my sin! I recognize my faults; I am always conscious of my sins. I have sinned against you—only against you—and done what you consider evil... Remove my sin, and I will be clean; wash me, and I will be whiter than snow... Create a pure heart in me, O God, and put a new and loyal spirit in me.[29]

Alan, I do hope your friend can read the whole of Psalm 51, and use some of the beautiful words there to help her speak to God about her own sin.

The final section of your letter points to the biggest part of your friend's current problem. She slept with this person she met, felt awful about having committed a sin, and since then she has discovered that she is pregnant. The first thing I need to say, Alan, is that that your friend should make sure she is 100 per cent certain about this. If a doctor has confirmed it, then we know she is pregnant. So ask her whether she has had definite confirmation—or is she just afraid that she might be pregnant?

Let's assume, however, that she is definitely pregnant and, as you say, she is desperate about the news and doesn't know where to turn. Well, one good thing to point out straight away, Alan, is that she has turned to you. You are both Christians, so I hope that through prayer and through what I can share, we can come up with a plan.

According to your letter, your friend is now asking you whether or not she should keep the baby. I take it from this that she may be considering either an abortion or continuing with the pregnancy and then giving the baby up for adoption.

Before deciding what might be the best course of action in this situation, it is worth looking at some of the teachings that I hold, which might be helpful for you both. Your friend may have made a mistake, but as a result of this we are now considering another life, and my teachings make it very clear that all life is God-given. As we read in the book of Genesis, at the very beginning of creation, '*So God created human beings, making them to be like himself. He created them male and female.*'[30]

There is also this passage from Psalm 139, which uses beautiful words to describe how God is intimately involved in the creation of all new life, and that he has a plan for everyone:

You created every part of me;
you put me together in my mother's womb.
I praise you because you are to be feared;
all you do is strange and wonderful.
I know it with all my heart.

When my bones were being formed,
carefully put together in my mother's womb,
when I was growing there in secret,
you knew that I was there—
you saw me before I was born.
The days allotted to me
had all been recorded in your book,
before any of them ever began.[31]

The ideas emerging here, Alan, are that every person is made in God's image and that all life is a gift from God and is therefore sacred.

I know that it must be a very tough time for your friend just now, but if she is pregnant the fact remains that all life is a blessing and gift from God. I know that your friend most certainly did not plan this, and so she may be feeling that she really does not want to continue with the pregnancy. But it is a new life. It is a miracle. It is God-given. If she continues with the pregnancy, in time the child may become a wonderful blessing in her life. Or she may decide to give the child up for adoption, in which case that child would become the miracle, the answer to prayer, that a childless couple has been seeking for years.

Alan, I hope I have been able to offer some advice to help you and your friend. Whatever she decides to do, remember that you can always come back to me for further advice.

God bless you both,

The Bible

Letter 8

Dear Bible, I have a problem. My name is Danny, and I'm in my second year at university. Over the last few months I have been feeling really low and quite depressed. There's no real reason I can think of to explain why I feel so low. I am a Christian and I do pray about it. I would like you to tell me whether there are any examples of people who were really depressed in the Bible and, if so, how they dealt with their depression. I'm hoping that by reading examples in God's word of situations similar to mine, I may understand why I feel like I do, and then perhaps work things out with the Lord's help. I look forward to hearing from you.

Dear Danny, I am sorry to hear that you have been feeling low and quite depressed. It's an awful experience to go through, and I hope that I may be able to offer you some words of advice and comfort.

I want you to know right now, Danny, that contained within my pages are the answers to all of humankind's problems. You may feel that life is pointless at the moment. Perhaps you feel that no one loves you or cares for you. Well, fear not! In your depression and despair there is someone who cares for and loves you more than you know. Jesus can change your life, Danny, and give it real meaning. You feel that life is nothing at the moment, but Jesus has said, *'I have come in order that you might have life—life in all its fullness.'*[32]

How encouraging those words are! Open your heart to Jesus. Let him heal you. Your are a person made in the image of God—think about that. Open your heart to it and realize that your life has a wonderful meaning: it has purpose and destiny.

Here are a few practical steps you can take, Danny, which I hope may help you to lift yourself out of these dark moods. First of all, you must decide that you want to break free from this depression. Where better to start than by meditating on the following words that I contain: *'Create a pure heart in me, O God, and put a new and loyal spirit in me… Give me again the joy that comes from your salvation, and make me willing to obey you.'*[33]

What a beautiful, positive start! I hope you find those words an inspiration. You mentioned in your letter that you have tried to pray about things. Well, you really need to commit yourself to this. I contain some wonderful verses that powerfully describe the effects of prayer and thanksgiving. Consider these two:

Don't worry about anything, but in all your prayers ask God for what you need, always asking him with a thankful heart.[34]

Why am I so sad? Why am I so troubled? I will put my hope in God, and once again I will praise him, my saviour and my God.[35]

What wonderful passages! Obviously a major cause of your suffering at the moment are the many sad, lonely or guilty thoughts passing through your mind, day in and day out. My next piece of advice, therefore, is that you need to renew your mind! Read what Paul writes in his letter to the Romans:

Do not conform yourselves to the standards of this world, but let God transform you inwardly by a complete change of your mind. Then you will be able to know the will of God—what is good and is pleasing to him and is perfect.[36]

Give your whole life and heart to Jesus, and follow his advice when he said:

Be concerned above everything else with the Kingdom of God and with what he requires of you, and he will provide you with all these other things. So do not worry about tomorrow; it will have enough worries of its own. There is no need to add to the troubles each day brings.[37]

Danny, I advise you to tell yourself from this moment on that you're going to take care of yourself and open your heart to God. Focus on him. You can conquer this depression of yours. Don't think that there is no way out, or that the situation is hopeless. As Paul writes in his letter to the Philippians, *'I have the strength to face all conditions by the power that Christ gives me.'*[38]

You write that you can't think of any reason for you to feel low, so I cannot offer advice on dealing with what might be the cause. But you also ask if there are any examples of depressed people in the Bible and how they coped with the problem. My answer to that is 'yes'! There are many examples. Perhaps, as you say, looking at some of these examples may help you to pinpoint what is getting you down.

Many people do not realize this, but probably the first examples of depressed people that I contain are Adam and Eve, the only two people to have truly experienced life in Paradise—and they both went and blew it! Getting kicked out of Paradise would depress anyone, but what else might have caused their depression? Well, it's the fact that they both disobeyed the Lord. You'll find, Danny, that in the teachings and stories I hold, this can be quite a common cause for people to feel low and depressed. They disobey the Lord, and therefore suffer from guilt, which can be a major cause of depression. Could it be that you are feeling guilty about something you have done, which is now really eating away at you, as guilt does? This is only a suggestion.

Let's look at another of my examples of someone who suffered as a result of guilt: King David, who committed adultery with Bath-sheba. You can read this story in 2 Samuel 11. It was only through confessing to God and asking for forgiveness that David could be released from the powerful grip of guilt and depression. We can read some extracts from one of David's Psalms, which demonstrates this.

When I did not confess my sins,
I was worn out from crying all day long.
Day and night you punished me, Lord;
my strength was completely drained,
as moisture is dried up by the summer heat.

Then I confessed my sins to you;
I did not conceal my wrongdoings.
I decided to confess them to you,
and you forgave all my sins.
So all your loyal people should pray to you in times of need;
when a great flood of trouble comes rushing in,
it will not reach them.
You are my hiding place;
you will save me from trouble.
I sing aloud of your salvation,
because you protect me. [39]

Many people find this a powerful passage, Danny, and I do hope that if this is where your problem might lie, you can confess to the Lord and feel his forgiveness releasing you from your guilt and depression.

As I finish my letter to you, Danny, I want to reassure you that all the wonderful teachings contained within me really will be able to help you. I should make it clear, however, that if you start feeling a lot worse in the short term, you must speak to some other Christian friends or counsellors who will be able to help you get to the root of the problem. You might even feel you want to discuss it with your GP, as part of the problem may be medical.

I wish you all the best.

The Bible

Letter 9

Dear Bible, my name is Fiona and I'm 16 years old. I've just started my A' Level course at school. I've had a really happy time in school over the years, but more recently things have been getting me down. I'm having problems with my mum and dad; we just argue all the time. I've felt so bad recently that I've taken to cutting myself, and pulling out hair. I just sit in my room and cry, and when I start to feel angry or really emotional, that's when I start cutting myself with scissors, my school compass, whatever I can find. I have been brought up as a Christian, but even my faith seems to mean very little to me at the moment. In desperation I'm writing to you for help and advice. Please, what can I do?

My dear Fiona, may I first say a big thank you for taking the time to write to me. It must have been very difficult, but I'm so glad you did. I believe this is the most important step in dealing with the pain you must be experiencing.

The first thing I would like to say to you, Fiona, is that you must contact your GP to arrange to receive some counselling; or maybe you know of a Christian counsellor through your church. Speak to your minister first, if you feel able to do so, and maybe they can point you in the right direction.

I can give you some help and guidance in my letter today, but I must stress that to sort out your problem with cutting yourself, and to deal with the terrible emotional pain you are going through, counselling will be a great help.

I don't know if you aware that today more and more young people are resorting to cutting themselves and self-harm, most of these being young women. You mention in your letter that it's when you're feeling really emotional that you start cutting and pulling out your hair. Well, it's a fact that those who turn to self-harm do so as a way of coping with difficult emotions. Like you, those who self-harm are unable to express their feelings openly, so they take out those feelings on their own bodies. Self-harming might be in the form of cutting, pulling out hair, burning, or even taking an overdose.

In your letter, Fiona, you don't say clearly what it was that led you to start hurting yourself. You mention that just recently things have been getting you down, and that you have started to argue with your parents a lot. A counsellor would be able to pinpoint the actual cause of your problem so that you could begin to deal with that. In general, some of the key reasons that lead people to cutting are bereavement, abuse, bullying, problems with money, and relationship difficulties. Perhaps you may be going through one of these experiences?

In the final part of my letter to you, I would like to share some teachings that I hold, which may help you along the way to recovery. I mentioned earlier that when you cut and harm yourself, this is actually an outward expression of the pain and hurt you feel inside. As a Christian, Fiona, you must know that God can see right inside us. He knows our pain. He understands those feelings of hurt, guilt, anger and so on that we carry around inside. If you let him, he will be able to help you. He will heal you. Let him examine you, as the psalmist says:

Examine me, O God, and know my mind;
test me, and discover my thoughts.
Find out if there is any evil in me
and guide me in the everlasting way.[40]

Another passage that you may find comforting is from Isaiah. All may seem dark and gloomy to you at the moment. '*The path you walk may be dark indeed, but trust in the Lord, rely on your God.*'[41] I think you might also find Psalm 23 very comforting at this time. I'll share the words with you here, so that you can meditate on them:

The Lord is my shepherd;
I have everything I need.

He lets me rest in fields of green grass
and leads me to quiet pools of fresh water.
He gives me new strength.
He guides me in the right paths,
as he has promised.
Even if I go through the deepest darkness,
I will not be afraid, Lord,
for you are with me.
Your shepherd's rod and staff protect me.
You prepare a banquet for me,
where all my enemies can see me;
you welcome me as an honoured guest
and fill my cup to the brim.
I know that your goodness and love will be with me all my life;
and your house will be my home as long as I live.

Fiona, I hope that my advice has been helpful. Open your heart to God. Let him heal your pain. Pray, and also get some professional help. All these actions will help and bring you comfort.

Eventually you'll be able to deal with the inner hurt, and this will stop the physical harm to your body, which is of course a temple: *'Don't you know that your body is a temple of the Holy Spirit, who lives in you and who was given to you by God? ... So use your bodies for God's glory.'* [42]

If there is anything else I can do to help you, Fiona, then please write to me again. I wish you well, and hope all works out soon.

With love,

The Bible

Letter 10

Dear Bible, I have a problem. My name is Harry, and I'm 24 years old. About seven months ago, I met a girl from Nigeria called Doyin. We fell in love and now plan to get married. We are both Christians. I am white and she is black. To many of my friends and family this has not been a problem at all, but my father, and some other people at my church, seem to think that I'm making a mistake in marrying Doyin. No one really gives me the reason for this, but I know for sure that it's because I'm white and she is black. What does the Bible have to say about this? Am I making a mistake, or should colour have absolutely nothing to do with it? What should I do?

Dear Harry, thank you so much for writing to me. I'm sorry to hear that you are experiencing some difficulties at the moment. I hope that I can share some good advice to help you.

First, I'd like to say how pleased I am that you have met somebody and fallen in love and plan to marry. I would like to wish you and Doyin every success for the future. That answers one of your questions, which was, 'Am I making a mistake?' You have met someone, you have fallen in love, you plan to marry, you are both Christians: I can't see any mistake there.

Sadly, though, when someone falls in love with another person from a different country and culture and they plan to marry, there are always people who just can't accept it. Parents may be heard to say, 'Oh, she is a really nice girl, but I don't think my son is doing the right thing.' Or some other family member might say, 'He seems pleasant enough, but it would be wrong for you to marry him.'

Whatever happens, it is going to be quite tough for you, as there are always one or two who just don't agree with 'mixed marriages', even if they can't give any valid reason for it. Some may say that it will be unfair to the children, and that as they grow up they may face prejudice.

You might have heard some people say, 'You're not just marrying Doyin, you know, but her whole family.' This is a silly argument, as all marriages involve the joining of two families. The point these people might be trying to make, though, is that you will be marrying into a totally different culture from your own, which might prove difficult for you.

Well, Harry, if you truly love Doyin, that will never be a problem for you. It may be a problem for one or two members of your family, and that will be something that they have to work out for themselves.

The key question, Harry, and perhaps the main reason you wrote to me, is this: 'What does the Bible have to say about marriage between different ethnic groups?' Very simply, the Bible does not prohibit this type of marriage or say that a person must only marry within his or her own ethnic group. The teachings that I contain are clear and simple. Every human being is created by God. *'From one human being he created all races on earth and made them live throughout the whole earth.'*[43]

Harry, I would like you to confront your father and the others in your church who seem to be opposing your marriage to Doyin. Do so calmly and positively, because we are working here to resolve differences, and you are all members of the same church.

Find out what it is that makes them oppose your wedding. Perhaps it is the fear that you are marrying into a totally different culture and a whole different set of values. Listen to what they have to say but, in the end, what you have to say in reply is simple. Doyin is a Christian girl. To you and all your family and church, she is a sister in Christ. There is no teaching within me whatsoever which states that you cannot marry this girl. The only teaching that does discuss prohibited marriages refers to the Israelites. They were forbidden to intermarry with pagans, and this was simply to help them avoid compromising their faith. It had nothing to do with ethnic purity, nothing to do with race. Non-Israelites who genuinely embraced the God of Israel were to be welcomed:

Do not ill-treat foreigners who are living in your land. Treat them as you would a fellow Israelite, and love them as you love yourselves. Remember that you were once foreigners in the land of Egypt. I am the Lord your God.[44]

Perhaps the most wonderful example of this is Ruth the Moabitess, who became the grandmother of King David, and thereby an ancestor of the Messiah.

At the end of the day, all you can do, Harry, is to show everyone how much you love Doyin, and that there is nothing anyone can do to stop you from marrying her. Ultimately, you have to remember what Paul wrote to the Galatians. Share this as a final thought with all your family who are having reservations at this time.

You were baptised into union with Christ, and now you are clothed, so to speak, with the life of Christ himself. So there is no difference between Jews and Gentiles, between slaves and free people, between men and women; you are all one in union with Christ Jesus.[45]

In your letter, you asked me if you were making a mistake. I hope you now have a clear answer to that question.

If you love this girl, marry her. You have the full support of me, God's word! Pray about the situation and meditate on the teachings I contain. That way, you can't go wrong.

I wish you and Doyin all the best for the future. May God bless you both.

The Bible

Letter 11

Dear Bible, I have a problem. My name is Helen, and I'm 16 years old. I have recently become a Christian, and this is a problem for my parents and family! None of them is Christian and they are all really concerned that I have accepted Jesus as my personal Saviour. They think I've become a member of some sect or something. They are always having a go at me, and the arguments are getting worse and worse. They are even saying things like, 'I suppose you think you're better than us now!' 'Why on earth do you want to go and become a Bible basher?' This is what I have to put up with nearly every day. What can I do? How can I continue to honour my parents as you teach?

Dear Helen, thank you for writing to me. First of all, I am delighted to hear that you have become a Christian and accepted Jesus as your Lord and Saviour. That's wonderful. What isn't so wonderful is the problem that this has caused between you and your family. A few verses immediately spring to mind when I consider your current situation.

Do not think that I have come to bring peace to the world. No, I did not come to bring peace, but a sword. I came to set sons against their fathers, daughters against their mothers, daughters-in-law against their mothers-in-law; your worst enemies will be the members of your own family.[46]

You have come to know the truth, Helen. You know that Jesus is the Son of God, and that through him you will gain eternal life. Your family have not yet come to realize this for themselves. They may feel betrayed. They may feel that they are not good enough for you, that you needed to find love and meaning somewhere else. Why on earth should you want to become a Christian? You now know,

Helen, that Jesus is peace and love, but your family do not know this yet. That is what Jesus meant when he said that he came to 'bring a sword'. At the moment, your family probably do feel like your worst enemies.

Sadly, this is what the Christian life is like at times. The verses above show Jesus predicting that following him is going to be tough. What is obviously troubling you as well, though, is how on earth you can follow teachings like the fifth commandment, *'Respect your father and your mother.'* [47]

There's also the advice that Paul gave in his letter to the Ephesians, which you may be finding tricky at the moment:

Children, it is your Christian duty to obey your parents, for this is the right thing to do. 'Respect your father and mother' is the first commandment that has a promise added: 'so that all may go well with you, and you may live a long time in the land.' [48]

Of course this is the way you should always treat your parents, Helen, but that does not mean it will be easy. You should treat them with love, talk to them gently, and let them see how being a Christian has changed your life for the better. Do not be drawn into any bitter arguments. Stay calm. Let them see the power of God at work in your life. If they ever genuinely want to talk about your faith, that's excellent. Use those moments to explain how wonderful it is to have a friend in Jesus.

Don't ever 'preach' to them, as that will only wind them up. When you can, share your faith with them. Continue to pray for them and for the whole situation. Ask the Lord to guide you in your words and actions whenever you are at home.

I hope that this does not happen, but there may come a time when a family member expects you to do something that you know goes against what you believe. On the one hand, my teaching is that you should obey your parents, but on the other hand, your parents may want you to do something that contradicts what Christ taught. In a situation like this, Helen, you would have to explain that, as much as you may love your family, you have to follow God's commands before anything else.

This situation is sadly all too common, and I appreciate how hard it must be for you. It is something that you are going to have to endure, but keep strong in the faith, read my teaching and pray daily, and just show your family Christ's love in action through everything you do and say. Eventually, you may see a change, and some of them may even turn to Christ, but at the very least they may come to accept that this is the way you have chosen.

I do hope that I have been able to help you in some way, Helen. Please write again should you need any further advice.

I wish you all the best.

The Bible

Letter 12

Dear Bible, my name is Jenny, and I'm 18 years old. I always hang around with a couple of girls, and we have been good friends for many years. Recently they have been going out a fair bit, meeting men and just sleeping around. They are getting a real reputation. The trouble is, I am also getting the same reputation because I hang around with them. I've heard some awful things being said about me simply because they're my friends. I have two big worries. I'm really concerned about their lifestyle and about the reputation I'm getting because of them. I do believe in God, but I desperately need advice. Please help me!

Dear Jenny, yours is a problem that I hear quite often. I'm sorry to hear that you find yourself in this situation. Firstly, you're really concerned about the lifestyle that your friends have chosen, and secondly, the reputation they are getting reflects on you as they are friends of yours.

Jenny, if your two friends are sleeping around regularly, and boasting about it, then I'm convinced that they must really have some sort of inner problem that needs dealing with. Perhaps they are feeling insecure, or they are desperate to experience love. They may be hurting inside in some way, and need some sort of help.

The other major concern, of course, is that they are certainly putting themselves at risk of contracting a sexually transmitted disease, even AIDS.

As a Christian, Jenny, the last thing you need is the kind of reputation that your friends are building up for themselves. You want to be known as someone who puts the love of Christ into action. I think that you really need to be taking some action here with your friends. If you are truly their friend, then you need to show them that you love them and are concerned for them. As it says in the book of Proverbs, *'Friends always show their love.'*[49]

Confronting your friends about their lifestyle will be difficult. They may not want to hear you. You may lose their friendship temporarily, or even permanently. But I believe that, in your heart, you know that you have no other choice. These are people you love, and they are putting their lives in danger and getting themselves the most awful reputation. Many men are going to see them as an 'easy girl to get into bed'. They will be viewed as nothing more than sex objects. Ask them if this is what they want. You're going to have to be quite harsh and upfront about it.

Perhaps they will open up to you and confide that they have underlying hurts or pains that are making them lead such a life. Perhaps they really do need to talk and would welcome you confronting them about this issue.

On the other hand, of course, they may not want to talk at all. They may turn against you. They may call you boring, or a prude. They may say that you are not normal if you don't go out, party and sleep around.

You can tell them that, as a Christian, you think sex is great. You can tell them that I, the Bible, think that sex is great too. I teach that sex should be celebrated. God's very first instruction to Adam and Eve was to go and have sex. He said to them, *'Have many children, so that your descendants will live all over the earth and bring it under their control.'* [50]

You can tell your friends that in the beginning, when God had finished creating the universe, he thought that everything, including sex, was good. King Solomon's poem, the Song of Songs, also celebrates love and sex. Make it clear, therefore, that being a Christian does not mean that you have a boring view about sex. What I do teach, though, is that while sex is a beautiful gift from God, it must be enjoyed in the right way. Sleeping around every week is misusing this gift. It's making it cheap and ordinary.

See how your friends react when you tell them what the Bible teaches and why you are so concerned for them. Tell them that their bodies are special and beautiful: *'Don't you know that your body is a temple of the Holy Spirit, who lives in you?'* [51]

Tell your friends that this is why you are so concerned. Remember, Jenny, if you are lucky you may get through to them, but maybe they will reject everything you have to say. But you are doing the right thing. The reputation you will end up with is that of someone who truly loves their friends and does their best to try to help them.

You will be letting them know how much you care, and how much God loves them. This is the most wonderful reputation anyone could have. If things don't work out initially, remember that in time, maybe even years, your friends will come to realize that what you did was out of real love for them.

I do hope that you will be able to get through to them, and if there is anything else I can do to help, please write again.

God bless.

The Bible

Letter 13

Dear Bible, I have a problem. My name is Simon, and I'm 43 years old. My problem is about knowing whether or not God actually answers our prayers. I've had good friends and family members die of illnesses over the years, even though I've prayed for them to be healed. Throughout my life I've prayed for various things and feel that I've never received any answers. This problem is really troubling me. Does God answer our prayers? Is there any point in praying?'

Dear Simon, thank you very much for taking the time to write to me. Your question is one that I get asked daily. So many people are desperate to know whether or not God really does hear their cries and prayers. I hope I can shed some light on this issue for you. I would also like to say how sorry I am to hear about the death of your friends and family members over the years. There is nothing worse than seeing those you love suffer illness and die, especially when you have prayed earnestly for them to be healed. I do hope I will be able to show that God does hear your prayers and knows about your pain.

The first verse contained within me that I would like to share with you records some words of Jesus, teaching that God does answer all prayer. Here it is: *'Ask and you will receive, so that your happiness may be complete.'*[52] It doesn't get much simpler than that! God does hear your prayers and will answer them.

Something that people need to bear in mind when they pray, though, is making sure that they pray correctly and in the right spirit. This may sound strange, but so many people simply ask God for things and expect to get exactly what they asked for.

A university student may pray, 'Dear God, please may I pass my exam tomorrow.'

They take the exam, and a few weeks later they find out that they have failed. The student then blames God, asking, 'Why didn't God answer my prayer?'

In your case, Simon (and I know how painful it must have been for you), you asked that God would heal those who were close to you who were ill and even dying. In each case, those loved ones did die. But in no way can we ever say, 'God didn't hear my prayer', or, 'It's God's fault that they died.'

It might seem so harsh when we pray for someone to be healed, and they still die, but sadly this is a fact of life. Young children die of cancer; a family dies in a car accident; the list is endless. Since the Fall, when Adam and Eve disobeyed God, evil, sin and suffering have been all around.

Jesus himself had to suffer and die to put things right again. Even before his arrest, he prayed and hoped that there might be a different way: *'My Father, if it is possible, take this cup of suffering from me! Yet not what I want, but what you want.'*[53]

Whatever it is that people ask of God, they must always add, 'If it is your will.' God will always answer prayers, but he does so in his ways, and sometimes these are not ways that we understand at first. This is explained beautifully in the book of Isaiah:

'My thoughts,' says the Lord, 'are not like yours,
and my ways are different from yours.
As high as the heavens are above the earth,
so high are my ways and thoughts above yours.'[54]

It is even the case that God seems to will suffering and death, according to some passages that I contain. This is a huge issue, such a mystery, with which many people have wrestled. We can do nothing but ask God, 'Why?' We can also just trust God. The whole book of Job deals with this problem superbly well.

Simon, I hope that some of this is helping you with your question about whether or not God answers prayers. In the great scheme of God's creation, there are reasons for everything that happens. To God, it all makes perfect sense. To people, it can often seem desperately confusing and unfair. But through praying to God and asking him to stay close to you, to guide you and fill you with his Holy Spirit, you will be strengthened, and slowly his ways will be revealed to you in your heart.

On the last day, when the trumpets sound and you enter his glorious presence, you'll understand at last the purpose of your life and all its experiences—what the 'big picture' has been.

I hope you also now realize why it is vital that you pray. It's your way of communicating with your creator. It's the way to pour out your heart to God, to feel his loving presence, to receive strength. Remember these words when you pray:

But when you pray, you must believe and not doubt at all. Whoever doubts is like a wave in the sea that is driven and blown about in the wind. People like that, unable to make up their minds and undecided in all they do, must not think that they will receive anything from the Lord.[55]

After experiencing suffering, many people turn to God and ask, 'Why?' They want answers. Instead of asking 'Why?', however, why not think of asking, 'What now, Lord?' God has everything under control, although it can be hard to remember this at times. Just pray to God and ask him to guide you and comfort you through the difficult times. He will always answer.

Whatever hard times you are going through, take time to pray—right now!—that you will sense God with you. Ask him to comfort you and guide you. As it says in Proverbs: *'Trust in the Lord with all your heart. Never rely on what you think you know. Remember the Lord in everything you do, and he will show you the right way.'*[56]

I do hope that these words have helped you, Simon. I hope you have learned more about praying to God, and that you understand that he will always answer you, even if it is not the answer you had expected.

I wish you all the best.

The Bible

Letter 14

Dear Bible, my name is Precious, and I'm 19 years old. Six months ago my parents were killed in a road accident. People have been very kind to me. Friends at church are helping me to come to terms with what has happened. My big problem is that I can't help feeling that it was a punishment from God. Is God punishing me? Why did this terrible thing happen? I feel so awful. Please could you help me?

My dear, dear Precious. I receive many letters daily, but your letter really did touch me. My heart goes out to you because of the pain and anguish you must be enduring at the moment. I was pleased to hear that you are receiving help and comfort from friends at church.

Some words that spring to mind are from the funeral service, where the minister says, 'In the midst of life we are in death.' Sadly, Precious, this is so true. We never know what will happen from day to day—and to whom. Losing your parents like this was a terrible tragedy for you. We can't even begin to try and explain it. There are no easy or immediate answers for you.

I am reminded of King David and how he felt during a time of suffering. Perhaps his words can relate somehow to you and the pain you feel:

Be merciful to me, Lord,
for I am in trouble;
my eyes are tired from so much crying;
I am completely worn out.
I am exhausted by sorrow,
and weeping has shortened my life.
I am weak from all my troubles;
even my bones are wasting away.[57]

Having gone through something like this, Precious, it is understandable that you want to question God: 'Why did you let this happen?' and so on. I dealt with a similar topic in my letter to Simon, about whether or not God answers prayers.

What saddened me a little when I read your letter was the fact that you asked if your parents' death may have been some sort of punishment from God. Let me tell you now, Precious, that the all-loving and merciful God does not work like that. Does our loving God deliberately give a two-year-old child leukemia and then kill the child to punish its parents? Does God decide one day, 'I think I'll make that plane crash and kill all 300 on board to punish their friends and family?'

Absolutely not, Precious. This is not the loving Father of whom Christ spoke. As a Christian, there is no punishment from God awaiting you, ever. Read Paul's words in his letter to the Romans: *'There is no condemnation now for those who live in union with Christ Jesus.'*[58]

I hope you understand what I have written here; your parents' death was not, I repeat not, a punishment from God. What happened was awful, and you will not truly understand why it happened in this lifetime. One day, however, God will reveal everything to you. In his great overall plan, there is much that does not make sense to us. In my letter to Simon, I quoted the passage from Isaiah that explains how we cannot truly understand God's ways:

'My thoughts,' says the Lord, 'are not like yours,
and my ways are different from yours.
As high as the heavens are above the earth,
so high are my ways and thoughts above yours.'[59]

Let your church friends continue to help and support you. Stay close to God; trust him; ask him to guide and comfort you. In the words of another of the Psalms: *'Trust in the Lord. Have faith, do not despair. Trust in the Lord.'*[60]

With love,

The Bible

Letter 15

Dear Bible, I have a problem. My name is Bill, and I'm 33 years old. I'm up at 4:30 every morning, I walk the dog, get back and have a quick coffee and then drive into work, which can take up to two hours with the distance and the traffic congestion. I work in a finance office. I barely get time to take a break or have lunch. I'm back home late in the evening, and I have little time for my wife and children. In short, dear Bible, I'm so, so stressed. It is becoming a huge problem, and I don't know how much longer I can cope. What can I do?

✤

Dear Bill, reading about your daily schedule, I'm surprised you had time to write to me!

Before looking at some of my teachings that may serve as antidotes to your stress, I think we need to discuss a few practicalities concerning your daily routine.

By far the most important words I read in your letter were 'wife and children'. You are going to have to make an urgent decision right now about what is the most important thing in your life. What should spring to mind immediately is 'my family', but, by the sound of it, they are the least important thing at the moment. If you think the stress is unbearable now, it will completely destroy you when your wife one day says that she can't cope any longer, and that she is leaving.

So, Bill, you need to make some big changes, and quickly, if you want to avoid a complete nervous collapse, or perhaps some sort of heart problem or a family breakdown. You've written and told me how you feel. Have you sat down and discussed all this with your wife? She is your best friend, there to support you through good times and bad, 'for better, for worse'. If you haven't done this already, then please do so. Perhaps you can look at the whole daily routine.

Is it always you who has to walk the dog? Why can't this job be shared? That would save you from having to get up so early. Just let the dog out briefly in the morning, and go for a long family walk with the dog later, after work.

You may feel that you are in a routine now, and you don't want to change. But remember, I don't think you have any choice. You are going to have to make changes for the sake of your health and your family.

You tell me, Bill, that your breakfast consists of a quick coffee. Another big mistake! From tomorrow morning onwards, you need to make time to sit down and eat a decent breakfast. Now that you'll be rearranging your dog walks, you will have time to eat cereal and fruit juice. Try to limit the coffee or cut it out completely. It only contributes to high blood pressure and won't help with reducing your stress levels.

Your journey to work sounds like a nightmare. Are there any changes you could make? Perhaps using public transport, or moving closer to your work? That way you'll also be home earlier and can have more time with your family. You also mentioned that you didn't have much of a lunch break. Another big mistake, Bill! No matter what the job, you must take time for lunch. Eat something healthy; make sure it gives you energy. Learn to forget about your work during lunch, because if you don't, your health is going to suffer. It's as simple as that. Find out from magazines and websites about healthy patterns for life and start following them.

I am now going to share some verses that can be an excellent antidote to your feelings of stress, Bill. These verses don't necessarily give you practical advice on how and when to walk your dog, or which route to take to get you into work quicker. What they will say, though, is that no matter how awful life gets for you, or how stressed you might feel, there is one place where you can go to find peace and refuge. Let me share some of these verses with you.

God is our shelter and our strength,
always ready to help in times of trouble.

So we will not be afraid, even if the earth is shaken
and mountains fall into the ocean depths;
even if the seas roar and rage,
and the hills are shaken by the violence.[61]

Read the rest of Psalm 46 and know that, whatever happens, *'the Lord Almighty is with us; the God of Jacob is our refuge.'*[62]

Bill, let God's love help you at this time. Give yourself to him, and let him carry you. Remember those wonderful words of Jesus: *'Come to me, all of you who are tired from carrying heavy loads, and I will give you rest.'*[63]

In the midst of your despair, cry out to God for help, and he will be there for you and your family. You could use the words of King David:

Hear my cry, O God;
listen to my prayer!
In despair and far from home
I call to you!
Take me to a safe refuge.[64]

My dear Bill, I hope I have been able to give you a few practical tips, and some helpful verses on how you should turn to God for help, and find refuge and peace in his love. In the words of an old hymn, 'Cast thy burden upon the Lord, and he shall sustain thee.'

Bill, I wish you all the best. Please write back if you want any further help.

May you sense God's peace surrounding you.

The Bible

Letter 16

Dear Bible, I have a problem. My name is Paul and I am 26 years old. I recently moved home with my family, and we have joined a new church. A week ago, my wife and I invited some members of our new church around for a meal. When they arrived, I asked them if they would like a drink, offering them wine, beer or soft drinks. They all made it very clear immediately that they did not touch alcohol. My wife and I continued having some wine throughout the evening, but we felt that our guests were judging us in some way for drinking alcohol. Before they left, some of them raised the issue, not in a nasty way, but hinting that they truly believed Christians should not drink alcohol at all. My wife and I thought we would write to you to get the final word on this issue. My question to you is simply, 'Can Christians drink alcohol?' I look forward to your advice.

Dear Paul, thank you for your letter. The topic of drinking alcohol is always a tricky one when it comes to what the Bible says about it. So many people ask me if it is all right to drink!

An immediate response is to consider John the Baptist and Jesus. John was very strict about what he ate—he was constantly fasting—and he certainly never touched alcohol. Jesus, on the other hand, drank wine; in fact some people even called him a drunkard.[65] Here are two people in the Bible: one drank, the other never touched a drop, but they both respected each other. It was not a problem between them. This is how it should be between fellow Christians. Everyone needs to decide for himself or herself whether or not it is right to drink alcohol.

What do I have to say about the issue? To be honest, Paul, I neither condemn the drinking of alcohol nor promote it. There are many passages contained within me that don't condemn drinking alcohol as such, but they do condemn drinking too much. Here is an example: 'Drinking too much makes you loud and foolish. It's stupid to get drunk.'[66]

This next passage is really good at describing the most terrible hangover. It clearly highlights the lunacy of drinking too much and the damage it can cause, both mentally and physically.

Show me someone who drinks too much, who has to try out some new drink, and I will show you someone miserable and sorry for himself, always causing trouble and always complaining. His eyes are bloodshot, and he has bruises that could have been avoided. Don't let wine tempt you, even though it is rich red, though it sparkles in the cup, and it goes down smoothly. The next morning you will feel as if you had been bitten by a poisonous snake. Weird sights will appear before your eyes, and you will not be able to think or speak clearly. You will feel as if you were out on the ocean, seasick, swinging high up in the rigging of a tossing ship. 'I must have been hit,' you will say; 'I must have been beaten up, but I don't remember it. Why can't I wake up? I need another drink.'[67]

Many people who have suffered hangovers have said that this passage from Proverbs is such an accurate description that the writer himself must have experienced it at some stage. Again, the passage is not condemning alcohol, Paul, but the misuse of it.

There are many other passages that teach similar lessons. Another example comes from Paul's letter to the Ephesians, which again condemns the misuse of wine: 'Do not get drunk with wine, which will only ruin you.'[68]

But I would now like to share with you some verses that sound quite positive about alcohol. In the book of Genesis, you can read the following: 'And Melchizedek, who was king of Salem and also a priest of the Most High God, brought bread and wine to Abram, blessed him, and said, "May the Most High God, who made heaven and earth, bless Abram!"'[69] Here we have Melchizedek, who is seen as a type of 'Christ-like' character in the Old Testament, offering wine to Abraham as a gift.

If the drinking of wine is forbidden and considered a sin, then it seems a little strange that Jesus' first miracle was to turn water into wine at a wedding in Cana. He not only provided the best wine the guests had ever tasted, but he supplied it in vast quantities, as much as 600 litres![70]

In the apostle Paul's letter to Timothy, he gives the following advice: *'Do not drink water only, but take a little wine to help your digestion, since you are ill so often.'*[71]

There is no condemnation of wine here—in fact, the opposite. Timothy was being encouraged to drink a little wine to help him. I know that scientists today, Paul, say that drinking a little red wine each day can actually be very beneficial Timothy was getting the same advice, even back then.

Another amazing passage that really does seem to encourage the drinking of wine and beer comes from the book of Deuteronomy:

Sell your produce and take the money with you to the one place of worship. Spend it on whatever you want—beef, lamb, wine, beer—and there, in the presence of the Lord your God, you and your families are to eat and enjoy yourselves.[72]

This could apply to a family having a good pub lunch after church on a Sunday!

The writer of Psalm 104 thanks God for many things, including wine that makes him happy: *'You make grass grow for the cattle and plants for human beings to use, so that they can grow their crops and produce wine to make them happy.'*[73]

Another verse from the book of Deuteronomy suggests that wine is a blessing from God: *'He will love you and bless you, so that you will increase in number and have many children; he will bless your fields, so that you will have corn, wine, and olive oil.'*[74]

I contain many more passages suggesting that wine is a gift and blessing from God. This gift, like any gift from God, is to be enjoyed but not abused. During the Passover festival, it was and still is today customary to drink four glasses of wine during the celebration. Jesus and his disciples would certainly have done this during the Last Supper. Of course, wine is also a special symbol for Christians, representing the blood of Christ, that you share in the communion service.

I hope you're getting the picture now, Paul. As a Christian, if you choose to drink wine or beer, or any alcohol, it is acceptable according to my teachings. It all comes down to individual choice, and we should respect each other's choice.

If you enjoy your wine or beer, then continue to do so. Abusing it is a different story. For people who feel that they can't drink moderately, then it is a real problem and they shouldn't touch alcohol at all. But if you can enjoy some wine at meal times, or a few beers with friends and family, then that's wonderful.

I do hope this answers your question, Paul. Should you have any further questions on this issue, please write to me again.

May God fill your heart with joy and peace.

The Bible

Letter 17

Dear Bible, my name is Zoë, I am 43 years old, and I have a problem that is tearing me apart. My mother Mary is 72 years old and is very seriously ill. Her body is riddled with cancer. She is in continual pain and I am told that she faces a fairly long drawn-out death. The hospital doctors and nurses are doing a fine job, although my mother is back home again at the moment. My problem is this. Just recently, my mother asked me if we could travel to Holland or Switzerland and arrange to have euthanasia. She said she was terribly unhappy, in a lot of pain, and would now like to die. She told me that if I truly loved her, I would respect this wish. She says that she wants to die with dignity. Having people feed her, help her go to the toilet and wash every day is not what she considers 'living'.

I feel it would be wrong to do this, but she desperately wants me to grant her wish. She begs me every day, and tells me that it would be the most loving and caring thing to do. I desperately need some advice, and look forward to your reply.

Dear Zoë, thank you for your letter. I am so sorry to hear about your mother Mary. The pain she is going through must be unbearable, and it must be extraordinarily difficult for you to see her suffer like this.

The issue of euthanasia that you raise in your letter is so controversial today. We will need to examine some of my key teachings that deal with the whole issue of suffering, and the right to take a life, even if it is to help someone who is suffering.

The pressure that you are now under must feel like a thousand tons! Here is your dear mother, whom you love so much, suffering and dying of a dreaded disease. That's bad enough, but to have her ask you to help her die, to end her suffering, is a whole new matter.

If you were to do this in the UK, you would be found guilty of murder, but as you mention in your letter, other countries, such as Holland and Switzerland, do allow euthanasia.

There are some Christians who believe that the UK law should be changed. They argue that God wants all people to have quality of life, and if someone does not have this quality of life because of a terrible illness, then maybe euthanasia could be an option. Some Christians also argue that whatever we do in life should be done out of love. They go on to argue that if someone is suffering and they ask you to let them die in dignity, you should allow that if you truly love them.

So you see, Zoë, this is a very contentious area. You have written to me for advice. What I intend to do is to look at some of the many teachings contained within me that might relate to this whole issue. When we have done this, we'll look at what might be the best possible action for you in this case.

A key place to start is in the book of Genesis: *'Then God said, "And now we will make human beings; they will be like us and resemble us."'*[75] This verse shows that all life comes from God, which therefore makes all human life sacred.

In the book of Acts you can also read, *'In him we live and move and exist.'*[76] People only exist because God has created them. God is the author of all life. When considering euthanasia, one argument against it is that, as God creates all life, and all life is sacred, so no one has the right to destroy what God has made, for whatever reason.

One of the Ten Commandments clearly states, *'You shall not kill.'*[77] The word 'kill' here is more accurately translated as 'murder'. Many would argue that euthanasia is murder; somebody is deliberately ending another human life, therefore breaking this commandment.

The teachings within me also show that just as God creates life, so it is up to God to end that life in his own time. There are passages that clearly state that it is God who determines the length of an individual's life. Here is a verse from Joshua: *'But now, look. It* has been forty-five years since the Lord said that to Moses. That was when Israel was going through the desert, and the Lord, as he promised, has kept me alive ever since.'[78]

Then, in one of the Psalms you can read, 'He has kept us alive and has not allowed us to fall.'[79]

Reading these passages, Zoë, you can probably begin to see where I am going with my reply to your letter. Your mother Mary, who is suffering terribly, is asking you to end her life now, and let her die with some dignity. The verses that I have shared with you clearly point out that all life comes from God, which makes it sacred. It is God who decides how long a person is to live. Euthanasia, therefore, is interfering with God's plan, and many Christians argue that practising euthanasia entails breaking God's commandment, 'You shall not kill.' Euthanasia could be described as murder, which is the current view in UK law.

I know this is very difficult for you, Zoë, but the point I am making is that, despite your mother's desperate wish to die, euthanasia is not the answer, and would go against all the principles contained within me. I know she is asking you to do this if you truly love her, but there are other ways to handle the situation rather than resorting to killing her, albeit 'mercy killing'.

We will look at the options available to you later. Meanwhile, let's look at some other passages that help us to think about the issue.

In the book of Ecclesiastes, we read that God has appointed a certain time for each person to die: 'Everything that happens in this world happens at the time God chooses. He sets the time for birth and the time for death.'[80]

This verse makes the point that God has a plan for each person he creates. Shortening their life and shortening that plan through euthanasia interrupts what God wants to accomplish with that person. The fact that God has a plan for each one of us can be seen in the book of Jeremiah. God makes it clear that he had plans for Jeremiah to be a prophet even before he was born: 'The Lord said to me, "I chose you before I gave you life, and before you were born I selected you to be a prophet to the nations."'[81]

When we look at these verses, Zoë, we see that they really do suggest why euthanasia would be so wrong. It would be ending a life before God has ordained it. Despite the dreadful suffering that Mary is enduring—and I know this is difficult to fathom—there may be some purpose behind it all. This purpose is certainly far from clear at the moment, but one day, when you stand face to face with your maker, it will all make sense.

The question remains, then: what else can you do in this situation? You want Mary to be at peace, and to be able to die with dignity. Euthanasia is not really an option, but the hospice movement certainly is. Quite simply, this movement is considered by many to be the real Christian alternative to euthanasia.

A hospice is a place that looks after the terminally ill. Most pain can be relieved through the drugs administered there. When a loved one is dying, families may have many fears and questions about death and suffering, and the staff in a hospice are wonderful at helping them to deal with these issues. There is always a chaplain on hand, who will pray with you, help to allay any fears, and comfort you.

People may be worried about not dying with dignity, but this need not be a worry in a hospice. This might be the real answer for you and your mother, Zoë. I would urge you to discuss this option with your doctor. Let me share with you the following words, spoken by Dame Cicely Saunders, a Christian doctor and founder of the hospice movement:

I'm against euthanasia for a positive reason; I have seen people achieve so much in the ending of their lives—time that their families would have missed. It's often time after they might have asked to opt out, when they perhaps would have gone in bitterness, whereas they finally go in peace and fulfilment.[82]

Finally, have you considered the possibility that deep down, Mary doesn't really want euthanasia? She may feel that she is just in the way now, and thinks she might be able to spare you from having to look after her every day and watch her suffer. Mary may never admit this to you, but would you ever want to risk ending her life when it is not what she truly wants?

I do hope I have been able to give you some advice on this very sensitive issue. May God watch over you and Mary during this difficult time.

God bless.

The Bible

Letter 18

Dear Bible, I have a problem. My name is Roger. I'm a Christian and I'm married with two children. Over the last few years I have been spending a great deal of money on my family and on myself. I just wanted us to have the best. We have a nice house and a lovely car. My wife doesn't know, but I have borrowed a large amount over the last few years with credit cards and loans. My problem is that I am now in serious debt. I play the Lottery every week, hoping for a miracle. I'm really getting myself into a state about the whole situation. I'm so desperate that I sometimes wonder about ending it all. My family does not know about this, but they sense that there is something wrong, as I am just not myself. Please, please could you give me some advice?

Dear Roger, thank you very much for taking the time to write to me. I am sorry to hear about the stressful and worrying time you are going through. What makes it worse is that you're going through it alone.

There is a lot of teaching about money contained within my pages, which I will be sharing with you as I make a start on helping you to sort out your problems.

It's often hard to know where to begin with this massive topic. Many people worry about money. People kill others for money. People kill themselves because of money. One of the biggest problems to do with money is debt. This can be caused by many things: spending more money than we have, being cheated by others, losing money because of circumstances we cannot control, such as a fall in house prices or the stock market. Whatever the cause, it can make us desperate, as you are clearly finding.

Before we look at some practical advice, Roger, it is important that you face a few realities about your life. You obviously love and care for your family. You say you want the best for them. That's only natural, but at what price? When you say you want the best for them, are you only thinking of the best in terms of material things? You seem to feel that it is vital to have as much money as possible, to buy the best for your family and the best for yourself (you mention your lovely car).

You have borrowed a great deal of this money, and now you've even turned to gambling to try to sort out your finances. I need to point you to the warning that Paul gave in his first letter to Timothy: *'For the love of money is a source of all kinds of evil. Some have been so eager to have it that they have wandered away from the faith and have broken their hearts with many sorrows.'* [83]

You need to be honest with yourself before you do anything else, Roger. You have grown to love money. As a result, your heart has been broken and you carry around with you many sorrows, exactly as Paul wrote. You didn't mention it in your letter, but do you also find that you have 'wandered away from the faith'?

I'm sorry if this sounds harsh, but we need to start here before we can go further. Now, before I share some more valuable advice contained within me, let's look at a few immediate practical steps that you can take.

Roger, you are married. You and your wife have made vows to stick together through good times and bad, for richer and poorer. Therefore, you must tell your wife about the money situation. You said that she and the rest of the family have noticed recently that you've not been yourself. You must let her know the whole situation. Share the problem, although it may be a tough thing to do. You may feel embarrassed and ashamed. Your wife will probably be shocked at first, but I can tell you that she'd be even more annoyed if you let this situation continue without ever mentioning it to her.

Once you tell her, you'll start to feel better. Who knows but that your wife may immediately come up with a good and practical plan to help sort out the situation. Wives can be very good like that!

The first thing you may have to do is seek some professional financial help: someone who deals with debt-related problems. You'll be amazed at what excellent advice they'll be able to give you.

From now on, you and your wife will need to sit down and plan ahead financially. You'll need to discuss and write down exactly how much money you spend on everything over a week. You'll be surprised at how much this adds up. Compare it to the amount of money that you have coming in each week, and see how much you have to spare.

For the time being, only buy what you can afford to pay for immediately. Don't borrow any more money using a loan or credit card, which may have crippling rates of interest. It's worth mentioning that in my Old Testament, lending money at interest is forbidden.[84] This is a biblical principle that needs to be rediscovered!

As well as practical advice, Roger, I want to point you to God's help. Have a look at some of the following passages. More than anything else in the world, you need to know here and now that God loves and cares for you. Look at Jesus' words in Matthew's Gospel:

This is why I tell you not to be worried about the food and drink you need in order to stay alive, or about clothes for your body. After all, isn't life worth more than food? And isn't the body worth more than clothes? Look at the birds: they do not sow seeds, gather a harvest and put it in barns; yet your Father in heaven takes care of them! Aren't you worth much more than the birds?[85]

Trust in God, Roger. He will look after you, beause he has promised that he will do this. When you put your trust in the Lord, he will provide for you, but you'll need to understand that he will provide you with what you need, not what you want. Asking God for money and riches is not what the life of faith is all about. Instead you need to give your whole life to God. This will change the way you view life and money. You will look for happiness in the Lord and not in material things.

The riches that God gives you will be far more wonderful than any earthly possessions you could ever own, as these passages show.

Trust in the Lord and do good; live in the land and be safe. Seek your happiness in the Lord, and he will give you your heart's desire.[86]

Do not store up riches for yourselves here on earth, where moths and rust destroy, and robbers break in and steal. Instead, store up riches for yourselves in heaven, where moths and rust cannot destroy, and robbers cannot break in and steal. For your heart will always be where your riches are.[87]

Obviously the world you live in requires that you earn money to survive and provide for your family. That is common sense. Work hard, earn your money, but remember: from now on, any money you earn is not yours. It is always the Lord's. It is God providing for you. Live for God only, not for money and possessions. As Jesus said: *'No one can be a slave of two masters; he will hate one and love the other; he will be loyal to one and despise the other. You cannot serve both God and money.'*[88]

Forget the smart cars, and other expensive possessions. They will not make you happy. By loving such material things in the past, you got yourself into debt. When you truly give your heart to God, you will begin to understand what is important in life—and it's not money and possessions!

I hope that I have been of some help to you, Roger. It is a stressful time for you, but there is a very clear way forward. Please write straight back to me should you want any further advice.

God bless you and your family.

The Bible

Letter 19

Dear Bible, I am writing to you not so much with a real problem, but as someone who would like to have something clarified. My name is Alfie. I'm happily married with three kids. We all attend church regularly, and we are happy there. Some church members saw me coming out of the bookmakers the other day and they brought the topic up with me last Sunday after the service. I told them that I have always popped into the bookies a couple of times a week. I explained that I never gamble a great deal, and that I only put a few pounds on the horses in each race.

As we were discussing the whole issue of gambling, I also told them that I spend about £5 a week on the Lottery. This seemed to shock them even more, and they told me that, in their opinion, Christians should not gamble at all. I told them that my wife knew and that we didn't feel it was a problem, but they just kept insisting that it was a sin.

I fail to see any harm in it. Could you please advise me on this whole issue? As a Christian, can I place a little bet on the horses from time to time, or are the people at my church right in what they are saying? I look forward to hearing from you soon.

✣

Dear Alfie, thank you very much for your most interesting letter. You make it quite clear that as far as you are concerned, there is no real problem over your gambling. For some of your church members, though, there is a very definite problem. You're gambling and they think it is wrong for you as a Christian to do so. You would like to know whether or not their attitude is right.

With an issue like this, it is important not to go straight to a 'yes' or 'no' answer. We need to look at a few facts and then focus on what my teaching has to say on the issue. After that, we'll see if we can conclude whether or not gambling is a sin.

A good place to start is by taking a look at what is actually meant by the word 'gambling'. The common definition is that 'gambling' means to 'play or game for money or some other stake'. It can mean to 'hazard or wager'. It means to take some sort of calculated risk for monetary or personal gain.

Some would say that just looking at these definitions is cause enough for worry. The idea of 'hazard' is a little off-putting. There is definitely a strong element of uncertainty where gambling is involved. You could end up losing a great deal.

To some people, this is a real worry. To others, the whole thrill of it all is the reason why they gamble. Will they win and end up with more than they started with, or will they lose everything? It can be a real buzz—so much so that you can easily become addicted. Then it becomes a compulsion. When you get to this stage, you can't stop unless you receive professional help. There are millions of people all over the world who are quite simply addicted to gambling. Many will deny that they have such a problem, but when you try getting them to stop, it's impossible.

Along with the addiction, which is serious enough, come all the debts. People can owe thousands or even hundreds of thousands of pounds. This can ruin families. Some borrow money from un-scrupulous lenders, end up losing it all and then even find that their lives are in danger when they can't pay it back.

This all sounds quite harsh, Alfie, and you're probably thinking, 'What has all this got to do with me?' To be honest, you may be partly right. You'll probably never end up in such a mess, but it is still what gambling does to many people. Although it may never happen to you, such harm can never be entirely ruled out. This is the danger of gambling, and this is probably the basis of your church friends' anxiety. They clearly feel that, as a Christian, you must be seen as having nothing to do with such a dangerous activity.

A key teaching, which may well be on their minds, comes from Paul's first letter to the Corinthians:

Well, whatever you do, whether you eat or drink, do it all for God's glory. Live in such a way as to cause no trouble either to Jews or Gentiles or to the church of God. Just do as I do; I try to please everyone in all that I do, not thinking of my own good, but of the good of all, so that they might be saved. Imitate me, then, just as I imitate Christ.[89]

Because of the real dangers of gambling, your church friends are concerned that you might be leading others astray, even though you don't mean to do so. To them, a Christian coming out of the bookies is not setting a good example.

I think you might have a clue now as to where my advice is tending. To you, gambling may just be a bit of fun, but it has destroyed millions of lives. You say in your letter that you also do the Lottery every week. Many people do the Lottery because they want to be rich and no longer wish to work. These reasons go totally against the teachings contained within me. Let me share some of them with you, Alfie.

Many people gamble because of greed. Rather than working and earning an honest living, they gamble: they want that money! As I said also in my letter to Roger, Paul's teaching says it all: *'For the love of money is a source of all kinds of evil. Some have been so eager to have it that they have wandered away from the faith and have broken their hearts with many sorrows.'*[90]

This verse could have been written purely for gamblers! Many of those who gamble out of greed are totally ignoring this important biblical principle.

My teaching make it clear that there is only one way to 'get ahead' in life and that is through hard work. There are many passages contained within me that make this point. In the book of Genesis, it says, *'Then the Lord God placed the man in the Garden of Eden to cultivate it and guard it.'*[91] God says in the Ten Commandments, *'You have six days in which to do your work, but the seventh day is a day of rest dedicated to me.'*[92]

Then there is Paul's advice to all those who were lazy in the time of the early church: *'Whoever refuses to work is not allowed to eat.'*[93] And what about that wonderful passage in the book of Proverbs:

Lazy people should learn a lesson from the way ants live. They have no leader, chief, or ruler, but they store up their food during the summer, getting ready for winter. How long is the lazy man going to lie in bed? When is he ever going to get up? 'I'll just take a short nap,' he says; 'I'll fold my hands and rest a while.' But while he sleeps, poverty will attack him like an armed robber.[94]

Quite simply, work is a divinely ordained activity. The idea of wanting to win the Lottery and give up work goes against all that God wants from and for people.

Your friends at church are also concerned about how gambling may be affecting your relationship with God. You are playing games of chance in order to try to provide yourself with a little extra. In doing so, you can end up losing a lot. As a Christian, your trust should be in God's ability to provide for you. Read carefully what Jesus says in Matthew's Gospel:

Do not start worrying: 'Where will my food come from? Or my drink? Or my clothes?' (These are the things the pagans are always concerned about.) Your Father in heaven knows that you need all these things. Instead, be concerned above everything else with the Kingdom of God and with what he requires of you, and he will provide you with all these other things. So do not worry about tomorrow; it will have enough worries of its own. There is no need to add to the troubles each day brings.[95]

Forget about your gambling, Alfie. Forget about trying to provide yourself with a little extra for tomorrow. I know your gambling is not a serious problem for you compared to many other people, but you are still hoping for that 'big win'. You don't need to have to do this. God will provide for all your needs.

I also contain teachings about what is meant by being 'truly rich'. True riches are always spiritual. You can be rich in Christ's glory, rich in faith, rich in good deeds and in mercy. Paul writes to Timothy, *'Religion does make a person very rich, if he is satisfied with what he has.'*[96]

Alfie, I advise you to stop the gambling as soon as you can, just in case it becomes a problem one day. Do you want to take that chance? Don't gamble on this! Those who do gamble seriously can end up robbing their own family to feed their addiction. Heed the warning in the book of Proverbs: *'If you try to make a profit dishonestly, you will get your family into trouble. Don't take bribes and you will live longer.'*[97]

Even a few small bets on the horses is not a good idea. As a Christian, you need to shine like a light in the world. You need to set an example to others about what it means to live the Christian life. If people see you coming out of the bookmakers regularly, then they will think that gambling is fine, even for Christians.

Your friends at church meant no harm when they brought up this topic with you. They love you as a brother in Christ. They weren't judging you, but wanted you to know the real dangers of gambling. It would be great if you could talk to them again on Sunday and let them know what you have learnt.

If you happen to know people who do gamble seriously and have got themselves into trouble, perhaps you could offer them help and friendship. Find out where they might get some counselling, and let them know that they can discuss their problem with you. Now that you know the dangers, it would be wonderful if you could help or warn others.

Alfie, I know you didn't really have a problem as such, but at least you now know the answer to your question: as a Christian, you shouldn't gamble. Set an example. Make a stand for Christ.

God bless and keep you.

The Bible

Letter 20

Dear Bible, my name is Leona, and I am 15 years old. I was confirmed last year, and I love my church. I am very happy as a Christian, and I have many good friends at school. Over the last few months, though, I have begun getting into a bit of trouble at school. Nothing serious, but my form tutor phoned my parents last week, telling them that I was starting to get involved in silly behaviour—things like being cheeky to some of the teachers, turning up late to lessons and not paying attention in class. My parents were very disappointed. The problem is that some of my friends want me to get involved in stuff I know is wrong, but I don't want to let them down. I don't want to lose their friendship. Some of them have started smoking, and one or two of them are smoking cannabis. They want me to smoke, and sneak out to their friends' parties at the weekend, where I've heard there is a lot of alcohol and also other drugs. I feel pressured and don't know what to do. My faith is important to me, but at the same time these people have been my friends for years. I feel that I don't want to let them down or lose them. What should I do?

Dear Leona, I am glad that you have taken the time to write to me. First of all, I am delighted to hear that you were recently confirmed, that you love your church, and that you are so happy being a Christian. This is good news, and you'll find out later in my letter how important all this can be in your life.

I am sorry, though, that you're going through a difficult time at the moment. It must be hard for you to see your parents' disappointment. You obviously come from a loving home, a truly Christian home. Your parents care about you a great deal, and want the best for you.

Being a pupil at school, you will have heard the expression 'peer pressure' many times. But in your case, Leona, it's not just a matter of learning about what the phrase means. You're facing some pretty tough peer pressure in reality, and you don't know what to do.

The dilemma you're facing is this: if you give in to the peer pressure, you'll get into more trouble and you'll feel guilty; if you don't give in, though, you'll avoid getting into trouble or feeling guilty, but you'll be afraid of losing your friends. What are you to do? Let's get down to sorting out this problem.

As a Christian, Leona, I'm sure you've heard about the Devil or Satan, and what a cunning deceiver he is. Well, he's deceiving you right now. He doesn't like the fact that you're a Christian, but I think he's quite happy with the way many of your friends are behaving—getting into trouble, doing drugs. Satan loves all that! What he doesn't like is the fact that you believe in God. You have accepted Jesus Christ as your Saviour. Satan will do everything he can to ruin this for you. Each time your friends want you to misbehave, or smoke, or start going to these parties where even more could go wrong, it's as if the Devil is tempting you to go against what you know, deep down, to be right.

Is this what you want, Leona? Do you want to stay on the path with God or be led astray by your friends? It is a hard question to face, and I understand how important your friends are for you, but you are going to have to make a decision. The most important thing you have to remember is that God is with you.

Here are some verses that you should learn off by heart, and say to yourself when you feel you are being tempted. '*So then, submit to God. Resist the Devil, and he will run away from you. Come near to God, and he will come near to you.*'[98]

I know it will be hard for you, but next time your friends want you to join in with something that you, as a Christian, know is wrong, you'll have to tell them that you don't want to do it. If they want to know why, don't be ashamed of the truth. Just tell them that as a Christian you don't want to be involved in those activities. Ask them to respect your beliefs.

It will be hard to do this at first, as you'll be wondering how they might react. Some of your friends might be quite impressed at how you're sticking to your principles and your faith. Others might just laugh at you. Remember, though, to stick to what you know is right.

You may end up losing some friends, but they'll be the ones who will just get into more and more serious trouble. You do not want to bring this on yourself or your family.

You also should remember, Leona, that even Jesus was tempted by the Devil, but he resisted. Actually, on each of the three occasions that he resisted, he quoted parts of me. You can read about Jesus' temptation in Matthew's Gospel, chapter 4, verses 1 to 11.

You could also read the book of Job, Leona. Here you will discover how Satan tempted Job, to test his faith in God, but Job resisted. He knew what was right. Despite the disasters that Job experienced, he was still able to say, *'God is so wise and powerful; no one can stand up against him… Though I am innocent, all I can do is beg for mercy from God my judge.'* [99]

Like I said, Leona, it will be hard for you, but God has promised never to lead us into situations where the temptation is too hard to bear. Look what Paul writes in his first letter to the Corinthians:

Every test that you have experienced is the kind that normally comes to people. But God keeps his promise, and he will not allow you to be tested beyond your power to remain firm; at the time you are put to the test, he will give you the strength to endure it, and so provide you with a way out. [100]

What great words! When your friends tempt you to do something you know to be wrong, God will give you the power to resist.

The final verse I want to share with you is one that you should already know by heart. It's part of the Lord's Prayer, which you may well say every week at church. Next time you say the prayer, focus on this part: *'Do not bring us to hard testing, but keep us safe from the Evil One.'* [101] You may know the words as, 'Lead us not into temptation, but deliver us from evil.'

Well, Leona, I do hope my advice has been helpful and that you now know what to do about the peer pressure you are enduring. Just remember that God is with you every step of the way.

God bless and keep you safe.

The Bible

Letter 21

Dear Bible, my name is Alex, and I am 15 years old. I need to know whether I have a problem or not. I've not been able to talk about this with anyone, and I find it very embarrassing even writing to you. My family is Christian, and we are a close family, but I'm afraid I can't discuss this one issue even with them. The thing is, I have recently started masturbating. Part of me thinks it's OK to do this, and yet I feel that as a Christian I am doing something very wrong. I feel I might be committing some major sin. As I say, I can't discuss this with anyone, and I desperately need to know whether masturbation is wrong for Christians. Please write back soon. Thanks.

My dear Alex, first of all, may I say 'well done' for writing to me. Masturbation has always been one of those topics that people don't want to discuss with anyone. You'll be surprised at how many people want advice on this topic, and not just teenagers.

As far as your parents are concerned, let me make you instantly feel a bit more at ease: they too have probably masturbated in their lifves, and it wouldn't surprise me if they have already guessed that you have started doing it as well.

Masturbation is a strange topic. Nearly everyone has done it and yet it's something that no one ever talks about.

You're probably worried because, the few times that you have heard people talking about the subject, it comes across as something dirty. You may have heard it mentioned at a church youth group. Maybe it was described as a sin. On the other hand, I know that when schools teach sex education, one of the topics discussed is masturbation, and most schools will explain that it is simply part of growing up. Youngsters may be told that it is only natural to start exploring their bodies as they get older.

Before we look at the rights and wrongs of this issue, bear in mind that, as a teenager, it is quite normal for you to start masturbating and exploring the sexual side of your body. But we need to get down to answering your key question: is it a sin for a Christian to masturbate? Let us look at what my teaching says on the whole matter—although, in fact, I say little about masturbation as such.

There is one passage contained within me that some have used to argue against masturbation:

But Onan knew that the children would not belong to him, so whenever he had intercourse with his brother's widow, he let the semen spill on the ground, so that there would be no children for his brother. What he did displeased the Lord, and the Lord killed him also.[102]

Although some people have tried to argue from this passage that masturbation is wrong, it's clearly nothing to do with it. This passage is about one man trying to fix which of his wives will give birth to the first son and heir of the family. This clearly went against what the Lord God wanted, and challenged his authority. The story has nothing to do with Onan masturbating and wasting his 'seed'. He did not do what was expected of him, and it was an awful way to treat the woman. Apart from this passage, I contain no other verses that can even remotely be identified as dealing with masturbation directly.

The kind of people who used the story of Onan as an argument against masturbation were also those who believed that the only right reason for having sex was to produce children. Once upon a time, Alex, not only was masturbation never discussed, but people hardly ever talked about sex. And when sex was discussed, no one would ever describe it as pleasurable.

Well, you only have to read the book in me called The Song of Songs (or Song of Solomon) to discover that sex is about pleasure. Read this book, Alex. The beauty and wonder and satisfaction of sex are described in wonderful poetry. Sex is a gift from God, and if it's kept within marriage, it's perfect. Not once does the Song of Songs mention that sex is only for conceiving children.

Other people have argued that although masturbation may not be explicitly mentioned in the Bible, it is possible to deduce that it is indeed a sin, in the same way that taking heroin, dropping nuclear bombs and so on are clearly wrong although not actually condemned. That is a fair point, but it can't be applied to masturbation. This is not a modern phenomenon! The question that needs to be asked is this: why did God give so many laws and restrictions about different sexual activities, while saying nothing about masturbation? There are laws about adultery, fornication, who you can and can't have sex with, laws about sex with animals; the list goes on, but masturbation is not mentioned.

I mentioned earlier, Alex, that in your sex education lessons at school, you were probably told that young people start exploring their own bodies as they begin to develop sexually. For many youngsters, this usually means that they start masturbating. They suddenly discover a wonderful part of this body that God has given them. So far, you might be thinking that this all sounds quite straightforward. There's nothing in the Bible about masturbation, so what's the problem?

Now have to ask another question, however: is there a time when masturbation can become a serious problem, a sin?

Masturbation does become a sin, Alex, when those doing it resort to looking at any form of pornography, whether it's magazines, videos or pictures on the Internet. If someone is masturbating and having fantasies about other men or women, this too is a sin. You only have to look at these words of Jesus to understand that:

You have heard that it was said, 'Do not commit adultery.' But now I tell you: anyone who looks at a woman and wants to possess her is guilty of committing adultery with her in his heart. So if your right eye causes you to sin, take it out and throw it away! It is much better for you to lose a part of your body than to have your whole body thrown into hell. If your right hand causes you to sin, cut it off and throw it away! It is much better for you to lose one of your limbs than for your whole body to go to hell.[103]

If you are looking at pornography when you masturbate, or fantasizing about anyone, then according to the above passage it would become a sin.

I would argue that the only time when fantasizing could be acceptable is if a husband is thinking about his wife or vice versa. When a loving married couple have to be apart for a while, perhaps because of work, and they have both discussed it as acceptable, masturbating and thinking about each other is seen by many as being healthy for the relationship. Some might also argue that if a couple are apart for a long period of time, one of them might find themselves in a situation where they are tempted to be unfaithful. The sex drive can be very strong sometimes. Masturbating is a way to release all that frustration. By doing this, someone can avoid the temptation to be unfaithful, and save their marriage.

There might come a time in the near future when you are tempted to sleep with someone or get involved in some sort of sexual activity. As an unmarried Christian, you should not do this. You should pray about it. If the urge is still really strong, physical exercise is a good way of releasing the tension. Sometimes, though, you may have to masturbate to release the frustration. Again, by doing so, you will stop yourself from engaging in some sort of sinful sexual activity.

Before I give you a final and clear guideline on this matter of masturbation, Alex, I want to deal with the health aspect, as there are so many ridiculous 'scare tactics' that are still used to dissuade young people from masturbating. Some still ask questions like, 'Does masturbating make you go blind?' or 'Will you go mad if you masturbate?' These ideas are nothing but nonsense!

In conclusion, Alex, let me summarize. You're a young man and you've started masturbating. Are you committing a terrible sin? Absolutely not, and don't let anyone ever tell you otherwise. You've discovered sexual pleasure, and it is wonderful. It is one of God's greatest gifts, one that you will probably come to enjoy in marriage. Remember, though, that you must not start having lustful fantasies, or looking at any kind of pornography.

Do not let masturbation become an obsession either, Alex. Work hard in school. Keep fit and active. Strengthen your faith day to day with regular prayer and Bible reading. Remember to tell God everything when you speak to him, even about your masturbating. He is the one who created your body and your sex drive.

Do remember that ultimately the beauty and enjoyment of sex are for marriage. That's what you should really save all your sexual enjoyment for. In the meantime, when a bit of pressure builds up and you just can't relieve it with that 'cold shower' or exercise, then it's fine to masturbate.

So, Alex, I do hope I have been able to answer your question satisfactorily. I know that it would have been hard for you to speak to anybody else about this. Thank you for being brave enough to write to me about such a sensitive issue.

God bless you, Alex.

The Bible

Letter 22

Dear Bible, my name is Natasha, and I have a problem. I am 14 years old, and I'm a Christian. The other day at church I heard the preacher say in his sermon that Christians should only listen to Christian music. He said it would be much safer for young Christians, in particular, to stick to Christian music, and not be influenced by some of the evil music and lyrics that are around. I was really troubled by this. I love a lot of modern music, pop and rock, and it's not Christian. I don't feel I'm being corrupted by it. Should I stop listening to my music and only listen to Christian music? I look forward to hearing from you soon.

Dear Natasha, thank you very much for your letter. I can imagine that, as a 14-year-old, you were quite devastated to hear that you can't listen to the music you love any more. I know how much young people love their music. There are music channels on TV, all manner of radio stations, magazines dealing with the bands and so on.

Let's look at Christian music, first of all. As a Christian, Natasha, I'm sure that one of the main aims in your life is to be as close to God as possible. It's a wonderful feeling when you know that God is near. You feel comforted and safe, strong and at peace. Well, the one real aim of Christian music is to help you feel like this. Christian music is all about wanting to praise God and get closer to him. It's as the writer of the Psalm said, *'I will praise God with a song; I will proclaim his greatness by giving him thanks.'*[104]

I don't know what style of music you like, whether it's pop, rock, rap, or whatever. The fact is that Christian music also comes in all these styles. You can go to Christian rock concerts; you can go to Christian raves. It's amazing. It's the style of music you love, and it's all Christian, praising God. Bear it in mind: Christian music can be wonderful.

There is no real advice contained within me about whether you should or shouldn't listen to non-Christian music. That will have to be a matter of choice. But I'm sure you are aware, Natasha, that a lot of modern music really does contain horrible lyrics. There are a lot of references to sex, to violence, to obscenity of all sorts. Of course there is also the risk of fans idolizing the stars, which could involve copying their lifestyles of drugs, promiscuity, hostility and so on.

Your preacher sounds as if he is aware of some of the unhelpful music that is around, and is probably just trying to protect you from it. But I wouldn't say that you have to take it to extremes. Be selective in the type of music you listen to, and do try some Christian music. There are some wonderful sounds out there, being made in the Lord's name.

As I have said in reply to other people's letters, your body is holy. Don't subject it to filthy, evil or violent lyrics.

Don't you know that your body is the temple of the Holy Spirit, who lives in you and who was given to you by God? You do not belong to yourselves but to God; he bought you for a price. So use your bodies for God's glory.[105]

With the Holy Spirit living inside you, Natasha, it's not a good idea to listen to music with obscene words, whether they're about sex and violence or even hell and the devil. Choose your music wisely.

Remember, though, that there is also much non-Christian music around that can evoke goodness and positive emotions in people. This sort of music is certainly fine and even helpful for a Christian to listen to.

I hope that this helps you, Natasha. It's great that you love music, but let the music you choose help you to grow; let it inspire you. Don't listen to rubbish that only fills your mind with images and ideas that might draw you away from God, who loves you so much.

If you need any more advice, just drop me a line.

May God fill you with joy as you seek to follow him.

The Bible

Letter 23

Dear Bible, my name is Tony, I'm a Christian, and I desperately need your advice. Last week I was contacted at work to be told that my father had committed suicide. He took an overdose. The whole family is devastated. My mother is still in a total state of shock. I can't even begin to describe how I feel. My father seemed happy, fit and healthy, and he was only 65. He left a short note saying that he loved us all, and that he hoped we would be able to forgive him.

At the moment, if anything, I feel angry with him for having done this to us all. I also feel guilty that I wasn't there to help him if he was feeling suicidal. I suppose that, as a Christian, I'm also concerned that he may have committed a terrible sin and now won't receive God's forgiveness. Please could you help me?

✣

Dear Tony, I am so sorry to hear your tragic news. I really do believe that surviving the suicide of a loved one is one of the most difficult challenges that anyone can ever face. Losing a loved one because of an illness or just old age is always a time of grief, but with suicide this grief can be intense, not least because of all those unanswered questions.

As I try to give you some practical help, Tony, and share some of my teachings, with you, I hope you will 'have hope through the... encouragement which the Scriptures give us'.[106]

As painful as it is, you will have to go through this grief and face the full force of the pain. It is not something that you can avoid or run away from. You have to pass through it in order to survive.

As soon as you can bear to do so, you have to face the fact that your father committed suicide. He took his own life. Many people who are going through what you are experiencing at the moment often avoid the real issue. Many don't even use the word 'suicide'; they can't face it.

You must let all your feelings out, Tony. Share them with family and good friends. These feelings may be confused; you may experience uncontrollable fits of tears, your emotions will be raw, but don't ever try to hide them. Don't fall into the trap of thinking that you have to put on a brave face. You probably feel like 'falling apart'. Well, do so, with your loved ones. All this is going to help you slowly recover and come to terms with the tragedy. During this time, remember also the words of Jesus: *'Come to me, all of you who are tired from carrying heavy loads, and I will give you rest.'*[107]

As well as pouring out your heart to your loved ones, Tony, you can also pour out your heart to your heavenly Father who loves you. It is with his help that you will find some comfort, and the strength to get through each day: *'The Lord is near to those who are discouraged; he saves those who have lost all hope.'*[108]

You write in your letter that you feel guilty that you didn't help your father. This is only natural. You and your family are all going to feel guilty, wrestling with such thoughts as, 'If only I could have been there for him', or 'Why didn't we see this coming?' Discuss these feelings with each other, and, of course, if you really believe you are guilty of anything, then confess this guilt to God: *'Let us have confidence, then, and approach God's throne, where there is grace. There we will receive mercy and find grace to help us just when we need it.'*[109]

Usually, though, in this situation, there isn't really anything you should feel guilty about. Of course it is natural for you to think, 'If only I had seen the signs, I could have helped him.' Eventually, however, you will come to realize that there was almost certainly nothing you could have done to prevent your father's death. You will come to understand that what happened was beyond your control. You cannot and must not blame yourself for what happened.

It is quite natural for people who are grieving to become depressed, especially someone experiencing such intense grief as yours. If you start to feel that you are withdrawing from others, that you just want to be completely on your own all the time, then you must get some help. A counsellor will encourage you to keep the grieving process moving. And remember, Tony, that in your despair you can cry out to

God at any time. He is always compassionate, and when we turn to him for help he will always answer us.

Another aspect of this situation is that you probably feel that no one can have any idea what you are experiencing, as it is fairly uncommon to have a loved one commit suicide. You may wish that there was someone around who really knows what it is like to go through this. If you do feel like this, I would recommend that you join some kind of support group for those who have faced or are facing similar circumstances. While no one's grief is exactly the same as others', joining a group of people who have all lost a loved one through suicide might prove helpful to you in your own grieving.

If one of the emotions you are currently experiencing is anger, then you must direct this anger in the right way. You can be angry with God, your dead father, yourself or others, but you must let this anger out. Go to the gym, chop some wood, find a quiet spot and scream; just release the emotion.

In your letter, you expressed the concern that, by killing himself, your father may have committed a terrible sin and may not receive God's forgiveness. One passage contained within me that might be troubling you is the following: *'From one human being he created all races on earth and made them live throughout the whole earth. He himself fixed beforehand the exact times and the limits of the places where they would live.'* [110]

Christians are generally agreed that suicide is wrong, based on the biblical principle that God has fixed our life span. If God gives life, then he alone is the one with the right to take it away. In the past, most Christians would have believed that suicide was a terrible sin. Some denominations regarded it as so dreadful that they would not bury suicide victims in consecrated ground. Nowadays, most Christians would agree that if someone is so desperate that they take their own life, they will not be judged for it—not by the God of love: he is a merciful and loving God who doesn't get angry easily.

Your father was obviously in turmoil moments before he killed himself. God would have felt his pain. And if, as the verse above says, God is merciful and loving, you can trust that your father will have been welcomed with open arms by this God of love. We will never truly know what was going on in your father's head to make him want to take his own life. Some say that for a person to take their own life, they must suffer some sort of temporary insanity, in which case they can't be held accountable for their actions. Today, we are more aware of the impact of mental illness and depression, and the God of love understands better than we ever can.

Tony, I hope I have been able to offer you some advice on how to deal with this tragedy. It's going to be a battle, but do fight on and work your way through your pain. Please remember Jesus' great commandment as recorded in one of my Gospels: *'Love your neighbour as you love yourself.'* [111] You really didn't have any choice or control over the suicide, but you must choose to take care of yourself now, so that you endure this awful time. If you follow my advice, read my teachings, and pray to God, you will survive.

May God be with you, Tony.

The Bible

Letter 24

Dear Bible, my name is Jane. I am a Christian, and I'm 17 years old. I am about to sit my A' Level exams, and, to be quite frank, I'm terrified! I have always hated exams, and I get myself in such a state, constantly thinking, 'Have I revised enough? Will the right questions come up?' I am also terrified of failing and letting my parents down. I desperately need to know how to cope with these exams. They are only a few months away. Please could you help?

Dear Jane, thank you for your letter. So it's exam time again? You won't believe how many people write to me regularly because of 'exam nerves' and fear of failure. I know it can be a very stressful time, and you are quite clearly finding life tough at the moment.

You may well be feeling that all that matters in life is that you pass these exams. I would say, yes, you should work hard and focus on your A' Levels, but there is something else that you should focus on more, and that's God. No matter how important you may think these exams are, it is God who should still be Number One in your life.

In your letter, you say that you are terrified. Well, I'm telling you now that you are not to worry, because that is exactly what Jesus says in one of my books:

Then Jesus said to the disciples, 'And so I tell you not to worry about the food you need to stay alive or about the clothes you need for your body. Life is much more important than food, and the body much more important than clothes… Instead, be concerned with his Kingdom, and he will provide you with these things.'[112]

Your faith in God is far more important than anything, Jane. Of course you need to work hard, but you do not need to worry. If you remain close to God, he will always look after you. Knowing that should help to calm you down, Jane. Remember these words from a well-known Psalm: '*I know that your goodness and love will be with me all my life; and your house will be my home as long as I live.*'[113]

In your letter, you write that you desperately want to know how to cope with these exams. So many students spend so much of their time worrying about the work they have to do that they spend little time actually preparing for the exam.

If you organize yourself properly, then the worry and panic will lessen. Many schools help students to plan their time well, by giving them revision timetables and good tips on how to study. Many teachers also give lessons in exam technique. Make sure that you use all these resources at your school. In Proverbs, it says, '*Pay attention to your teacher and learn all you can.*'[114]

There is no getting away from the fact that it is going to be hard work, but there's nothing wrong with that! I contain a verse that says, '*Whatever you do, work at it with all your heart, as though you were working for the Lord and not for human beings.*'[115]

During this revision period, Jane, you are going to have to make some sacrifices. Forget about going out with your friends every night, lazing in front of the TV and so on. It's time to get organized. It's time to work. You definitely need to make yourself a revision time-table, and you will need to stick to it. It is also vital that you have regular rests, not just throughout the day, but also one whole day off a week. If you don't get proper rest, you'll end up irritable and start getting in a state again. Make sure you learn all your topics, not just the ones you like. Any question might turn up in the exam, so you will need to be fully prepared.

Just before I conclude, Jane, here's a bit of advice about the day of the exam. Please make sure you have a good breakfast. It is very common, just before an exam, to start thinking that you have forgotten everything. Your mind might just seem to go blank. If this happens, it is totally normal, so please do not panic! When you are looking at the questions, your memory will be triggered and the relevant material will spring to mind.

When all your exams are over, Jane, just relax. Try to go away on holiday if you can. You will have earned a good rest. All being well, if you've followed my advice and revised hard, you should get the results you deserve. But don't worry about them for now. If you do need any further advice once your results are out, please do write back to me.

With love,

The Bible

Letter 25

Dear Bible, my name is Jack and I'm 15 years old. I'm a Christian, and I am in Year 10 at school, studying for my GCSEs. My problem is that all I think about is football. I have been told that I am a really good player, and I play for a top local junior team. My manager there tells me that I could become a professional player one day. I want to be like my hero, Wayne Rooney. My parents tell me they are a little concerned that all I think about is football. My teachers say that I am an intelligent boy and could do really well in my exams, but because I spend all my time playing football, I may not do so well. Is it wrong to focus on my football? I believe that God has given me a great talent for sport. Why can't I dream of being a top player?

Dear Jack, it was good to read in your letter that you feel that God has blessed you with a wonderful athletic ability, especially in playing football. It is wonderful that you have this skill, and you should make use of it as you are doing, but it should not be the only thing you live for.

Maybe you will be a professional football player one day, but that is some way off. It may not be what God has planned for you, and what you need to remember as a Christian is that God is in charge of your life. Look what it says in one of my books, Jeremiah: *'I alone know the plans I have for you, plans to bring you prosperity and not disaster.'*[116]

Please don't put all your hope simply into becoming a top-class player. It may not be what God has planned for you. You wrote in your letter that your teachers say you have the ability to do really well in your exams. Well, this sounds like another area of your life in which God has blessed you. You must not throw this chance away, Jack.

Another question you should be asking yourself is this: what would happen if you were to have a serious injury and could no longer hope to play professional football? This is quite a common problem. Many players suffer serious knee and back problems, and although they are not immobilized in their everyday lives, they are prevented from playing professionally again.

This is why you need to be fully prepared for life, Jack. You have got to study for your exams. That will please your parents and teachers, and will be good for you in the long run. You can still play football, but don't pin all your hopes and dreams on it. There are so many who share the same dream as you, but only a few ever make it to the top.

Listen to your parents, Jack. They only want the best for you—for you to be fully prepared for life.

Remember Paul's words in another of my books, Ephesians:

Children, it is your Christian duty to obey your parents, for this is the right thing to do. 'Respect your father and mother' is the first commandment that has a promise added: 'so that all may go well with you, and you may live a long time in the land.' Parents, do not treat your children in such a way as to make them angry. Instead, bring them up with Christian discipline and instruction.[117]

I also need to address why it is that you want to be famous. Is it the money, the fast cars, or what? If you are honest with yourself and do admit that this is why you want to be a famous footballer, then I have to tell you that, as a Christian, this is not what God expects of you.

You must not make these things the focus of your life or put your trust in worldly power, fame or possessions. In my letters to other people, I have shared these verses from the Sermon on the Mount, where Jesus refers to his audience as 'you of little faith' and says:

No one can be a slave of two masters; he will hate one and love the other; he will be loyal to one and despise the other. You cannot serve both God and money. This is why I tell you not to be worried about the food and drink you need in order to stay alive, or about clothes for your body. After all, isn't life worth more than food? And isn't the body worth more than clothes? Look at the birds: they do not sow seeds, gather a harvest and put it in barns; yet your Father in heaven takes care of them! Aren't you worth much more than birds? ... Instead, be concerned above everything else with the Kingdom of God and with what he requires of you, and he will provide you with all these other things.[118]

In conclusion, Jack, I would ask you to put your trust in God. Pray and ask God to guide you. There is always the chance that God may want to lead you into the life of a professional football player, to do his work and to be a role model for other young Christians. But that will be God's will, not yours. Work hard at school, keep enjoying the football, and always follow the advice of your parents and teachers.

May God be with you, Jack.

The Bible

Letter 26

Dear Bible, my name is Hannah and I am 16 years old. I am a Christian, and I'm just about to sit my GCSE exams. My problem is that I have no idea what to do afterwards. Should I take A' Levels, or some sort of vocational course? I need some advice! Most of my friends seem to know what direction their lives should take, but it worries me that I still have no idea about careers. Could you please help me?

Dear Hannah, thank you for your letter. I must tell you straight away not to panic. Many people just finishing their A' Levels still have no idea what they intend to do for a career. There are also plenty of people at university who don't know what their future plans are, so don't worry overmuch just yet!

Let me just quote from one of my books: '*The Lord has determined our path.*'[119] As a Christian, Hannah, you should remember that everything is in God's hands. He has a plan for you, even though you may not understand it yet. Speak to him daily through prayer, and read me daily. In time, you will learn what his plans are for you.

On a more practical note, it is your teachers at school and your careers officer who should be able to point you in the right direction. A careers officer is trained to ask the right questions and find out what your real interests and skills are.

If you are fairly academic, then it could be that studying A' Levels is the right choice for you. As to which A' Levels you should study, you will need to discuss this with your teachers. If academic study is not your real strength, then perhaps some type of vocational course is what you need to do as part of your sixth form studies. Again, it is only your teachers who can really help you here.

You also need to reflect on what special gifts God may have blessed you with. You need to pray about this, and speak to your friends and family, church minister or youth worker. Often it is those who are close to you who can spot such talents. You may be a caring person and a good listener. You may be very practical. You could be exceptionally skilled in organizing and leading others. Do ask God to guide you as you ponder these things. As is written in one of my books:

We have courage in God's presence, because we are sure that he hears us if we ask him for anything that is according to his will. He hears us whenever we ask him; and since we know this is true, we know also that he gives us what we ask from him.[120]

Although you may feel a little frustrated at the moment, because you have no idea what path to take, you should not spend hours worrying about it. After talking with your teachers, parents and friends, and to God through prayer, you will know which way to go.

You may have heard the word 'vocation'. It comes from the Latin word meaning 'call'. Christians believe that God has a special calling for every one of us. Whatever you end up doing, Hannah, it will be an opportunity for you to serve God and your neighbour.

I wish you every success for the future.

The Bible

Letter 27

Dear Bible, my name is Amanda and I am 28 years old. I have been married to John for five years. We are both Christians, and we have been happy together. We have two children—two girls aged two and four. My problem is this. For many years I have worked in an office, where I have made many good friends. About four months ago, I attended a leaving party. It was a really good night. Everyone was there, including one of my colleagues, called Steve. We have always got on well together. That evening, we had both had a fair bit to drink. We chatted for ages; and then it happened. I don't know why, but at one particular moment, it just felt right to kiss him. That night, I went to his house, and we slept together. He is a single man. I told John that I stayed with a friend.

That was four months ago, but since then, Steve and I have been meeting up occasionally for a meal, and I have then stayed over with him. I suppose, if I am very honest, I have to say that I am having an affair. I don't think John suspects anything. It has suddenly dawned on me, though, that this is all very wrong. I love my husband, and I have two wonderful daughters. I also love being with Steve, but I realize that it has to stop. As a Christian, I have committed a terrible sin. I feel so guilty! How on earth am I going to deal with this? Do I just stop seeing Steve, and carry on as normal, or do I tell John? Please could you help me?

Dear Amanda, thank you for sharing this problem with me and for being so honest. It is true that the situation is a mess, and it is going to be hard for you to sort it out. But I want you to know that I, God's word, will do everything I can to help you.

Before we focus on your problem, I must remind you that there is a great deal of teaching contained within my books condemning adultery, as I am sure you will be aware. The first thing it says on the subject is *'Do not commit adultery.'*[121] Adultery is the most widely condemned of the sexual sins. As I have just quoted, it is forbidden in the Ten Commandments, as well as being mentioned in the four Gospels and ten other of my books, including Proverbs: the woman who commits adultery *does not stay on the road to life; but wanders off, and does not realize what is happening*.[122]

You wrote in your letter that you feel so guilty, and wonder how to deal with the situation. That echoes what I've just quoted from Proverbs: adultery can destroy you as well as your relationship with your husband. I am not sharing these teachings with you to make you feel worse, Amanda, but I need to explain how serious a sin this is, which is why you are feeling so bad and why you are so desperate for some advice.

Jesus spoke of the dangers of adultery:

A Jewish leader asked Jesus, 'Good Teacher, what must I do to receive eternal life?' 'Why do you call me good?' Jesus asked him. 'No one is good except God alone. You know the commandments: "Do not commit adultery; do not commit murder; do not steal; do not accuse anyone falsely; respect your father and your mother."'[123]

It is so widely condemned in my teachings, Amanda, because adultery destroys marriages. A couple make vows to each other during the wedding ceremony, and an adulterer shows total disregard for these vows and for his or her spouse.

Your letter was a cry for help, however. You have committed adultery, and you have now come to see that what you are doing is wrong. You say that you and John have been happy together, and you have two lovely daughters. You have a great deal to be thankful for, and I have to be honest with you, Amanda, and tell you that this may now have all been ruined.

You wanted to know what you must do right now. You must definitely end this affair, immediately. Tell your colleague, Steve, that it is over. If necessary, explain to him that you are a Christian and that you realize you have committed a great sin. Tell him that it may have seemed like fun at the time, but you have put your marriage in jeopardy. You must make it clear to him that you love your husband and your children. If others at your office know about the affair, you may have to consider leaving your job as well.

And now to the most difficult part of this situation. You wondered in your letter whether you could continue as if nothing has happened, and never tell your husband about the affair. I think, as a Christian, you must know the answer already: *'Be kind and honest and you will live a long life; others will respect you and treat you fairly.'*[124]

That's my advice. You must be honest and tell John everything. This may well be the hardest thing you ever have to do. Your biggest fear, of course is how he will react, and whether he will leave you as a result. No matter, you simply must tell him. If you don't, the guilt will grow and grow until it actually destroys you.

At the beginning of this letter, I shared with you some of my teaching that condemns adultery. I would now like to remind you of the following passage:

[Jesus] went back to the Temple. All the people gathered round him, and he sat down and began to teach them. The teachers of the Law and the Pharisees brought in a woman who had been caught committing adultery, and they made her stand before them all. 'Teacher,' they said to Jesus, 'this woman was caught in the very act of committing adultery. In our Law Moses commanded that such a woman must be stoned to death. Now, what do you say?' They said this to trap Jesus, so that they could accuse him. But he bent over and wrote on the ground with his finger.

As they stood there asking him questions, he straightened himself up and said to them, 'Whichever one of you has committed no sin may throw the first stone at her.' Then he bent over again and wrote on the ground. When they heard this, they all left, one by one, the older ones first. Jesus was left alone, with the woman still standing there. He straightened himself up and sad to her, 'Where are they? Is there no one left to condemn you?'

'No one, sir,' she answered.

'Well, then,' Jesus said, 'I do not condemn you either. Go, but do not sin again.'[125]

Amanda, you have committed adultery, but you have realized that it was a mistake. Jesus does not condemn you. You have committed a sin, yes, but *'Christ Jesus came into the world to save sinners'*.[126]

In the passage I shared with you from John's Gospel, about the woman caught in the act of adultery, Jesus ends up by saying to her, 'Go and sin no more.' The question we have to ask is, 'Go where?' Well, the answer was that she probably went back to her husband and became the kind of wife that God wanted her to be. You are sorry for what you have done. Jesus forgives you, and he wants you never to do it again. You now have to hope that once you have told John about your adultery, he too can find it in his heart to forgive you.

Find a suitable time to sit down with John and tell him everything. Be prepared for him to be angry, maybe to storm out, to be devastated. Make sure you are able to tell him that you realize you have made the most awful mistake. Tell him that you love him more than anything and that you desperately want to be with him for the rest of your life.

It may be that you will want to write to me again soon, and let me know how John reacted. You may need further advice. It is difficult to say now how John will react. He may even react quite calmly at first. He may just want to cry and hug you, but then the anger may come later.

John will need to be given time to reflect on what you have told him, as it will be a huge shock. If he actually asks you to leave immediately, then you must do so. Stay with a good friend. While you are there, you could write a letter to him, reminding him how much you love him and that you will respect and understand any decision he makes.

In time, it may be that he wants to meet and talk. You are going to have so much to talk about that you may need to get some professional help, as well as talking to your church minister (if you feel that you can). You have caused a terrible fracture in your marriage, and you may well need Christian counselling to help mend it and make it strong again.

John will want to understand what made you want to cheat on him. What was wrong with your relationship? More than anything, he will want to know if he can ever trust you again.

In rebuilding your marriage, you will both need to start with the decision to commit to and work on it. As Christians, you will also both need to commit yourselves to the Lord and trust in him to lead you through the whole healing process.

It's going to be very hard, Amanda, and that's why I ask you to keep in touch should you need any further advice. You have most definitely taken the first positive step. You have realized your sin and, if you have confessed it to the Lord, he will forgive you.

Remember what Paul writes in one of my books: *'I have the strength to face all conditions by the power that Christ gives me.'* [127]

May you feel Christ's love surrounding you.

The Bible

Letter 28

Dear Bible, my name is Alice, and I am in desperate need of some support and advice. I am 29 years old, and have been married for two years now. I met my husband, James, at church about three years ago. So far, our time together has been wonderful. I thought we were both so happy. We talked about the future, and planned to have children.

Six weeks ago, I arrived back home from work. James was not there, but when I went into the living-room, I saw an envelope on the table with my name on it in his handwriting.

James told me in the letter that he had left, for good. The marriage was not what he wanted, and he had been thinking about this for quite a while. He told me that there was no point in trying to contact him. He said that this was the only way he could deal with things.

He explained that he had moved to a small flat somewhere, and not even his friends and parents knew where he was. He added, though, that he has not run off with another woman. He is on his own. Then, a couple of days ago, I had a letter from his solicitor: he wants a divorce!

Dear Bible, I am absolutely devastated. I've never felt so rejected, so lonely, so depressed. I do not know where to turn, what to do, whom to speak to. Should I hope that he might return, or do I just accept that he has gone, and try to move on? Please could you help me?

✜

Dear Alice, I would like you to know immediately that you are not alone during what is clearly a dreadful time for you. You are right to use the word 'devastated' at the moment. I do feel for you in this time of utter desperation, and I will share some of my teachings with you that I hope may begin to help you. I will also give you some practical advice.

First of all, I would like you to read the whole of Psalm 23. If you know a tune to this Psalm, you may just want to sing the words quietly. Given the way you are feeling, you probably have no real enthusiasm to read anything, but I urge you to take a look at this Psalm daily, or a few times during the day. They are powerful words, and they will start to offer you some comfort. Here are the opening verses of the Psalm:

The Lord is my shepherd;
I have everything I need.
He lets me rest in fields of green grass
and leads me to quiet pools of fresh water.
He gives me new strength.
He guides me in the right paths,
as he has promised.[128]

Let these words be the fuel by which you propel yourself through these darkest of days. In time, you will come to see what a great source of strength they are.

I would like to begin by helping you tackle what is probably your biggest question: 'Why did James walk out on me?' If a marriage had been a complete disaster, or there had been some sort of physical or emotional abuse, you might understand why one partner would just want to leave. But this was clearly not the case in your circumstances. In your letter, you wrote that he said he had been thinking about this for quite a while, and that marriage was 'not what he wanted'. For some reason, everything—not only being married but the whole of life—may have been getting on top of him and in the end he couldn't cope. We just don't know the full story.

Getting a letter asking for divorce must have been another huge shock. As a Christian, this must really concern you as well. You both made vows to God to remain married for life, or until 'death us do part'. Jesus clearly taught that *'any man who divorces his wife for any cause other than her unfaithfulness, commits adultery if he marries some other woman'.*[129]

Alice, you do not deserve to be treated like this. According to your and your husband's faith, the only grounds for him to get a divorce is because you have committed adultery. This is clearly not the case! I would suggest that you get yourself a solicitor and reply to James' letter, including this passage from Matthew's Gospel, and making it clear that you have not committed adultery and that you want to know on what grounds, as a Christian, he wants to divorce you.

My dear Alice, you wrote in your letter that you don't know where to turn or whom to speak to. May I suggest that you look 'towards the mountains', in the words of another beautiful Psalm:

I look to the mountains;
where will my help come from?
My help will come from the Lord,
who made heaven and earth.
He will not let you fall;
your protector is always awake.
The protector of Israel
never dozes or sleeps.
The Lord will guard you;
he is by your side to protect you.
The sun will not hurt you during the day,
nor the moon during the night.[130]

Turn to God. He has promised to help you. He will not let you fall. Let him guide and protect and comfort you through this nightmare.

If you have not already done so, discuss the situation with your minister. He or she will certainly be able to help you in some way. Remember that your church is also your family. Most of the members will probably be aware of your situation now, purely because James is no longer around. Many of them will want to offer you help and comfort. Some may have experienced something similar, and may prove to be a source of good advice and comfort.

This brings me on to something else in your letter. You wrote that you have never felt 'so lonely'. Well, this is hardly surprising, as you have lost your soulmate, your best friend. It's as if half of you has been ripped away.

One of my books teaches: *'A man leaves his father and mother and is united with his wife, and they become one.'* [131]

This oneness that Genesis speaks of has been destroyed in your case. This is why you feel so lonely. You feel like half a person. Your husband has gone, almost as if he has died. I am afraid there is no easy solution for this unique feeling of loneliness.

I can tell you one thing, though. This loneliness can actually become a pathway to God. The path might be quite difficult to find at first, but you can be sure that God will make it known to you when you turn to him with your pain.

The most comforting teaching contained within my pages is that you have a wonderful God who understands your emotions: *'Since the children, as he calls them, are people of flesh and blood, Jesus himself became like them and shared their human nature.'* [132] Jesus became human, and therefore shares in the full range of our emotions. Pour out your heart to him, Alice. Remember those comforting words of his recorded in the Gospel of Matthew: *'Come to me, all of you who are tired from carrying heavy loads, and I will give you rest.'* [133] Remember, too, that God has said: *'I will never leave you; I will never abandon you.'* [134]

Something else mentioned in your letter, Alice, was the question of whether you should wait and see if James changes his mind and comes back to you. One day he will have to come to terms with what he has done, and deal with whatever issue it is that troubled him. Meanwhile, however, I am afraid that you will have to come to terms with what has happened, and realize that he has gone.

Divorce is most certainly not the Christian ideal, but in a situation like this, it may end up being the only choice. Your husband has disappeared. At the moment, he wants nothing more to do with you. The one thing you can do, as you start to accept your changed circumstances, is to pray that God's healing power can work in his life as well as yours.

Remember more than anything, Alice, that God cares for you, so *'leave all your worries with him'*.[135]

Alice, I do hope that all works out well with you in the end. Please remember to write to me at any time, should you wish for any further advice.

May God comfort you and grant you peace.

The Bible

✣

Well that's all we have time for now. Thank you so much to all of you who took the time to write to me seeking advice. I do hope that I have been able to help. I also hope that those of you who read these problems and responses may be helped in some way in your own lives. Remember, *'Everything written in the Scriptures was written to teach us, in order that we might have hope through the patience and encouragement which the Scriptures give us.'* [136]

God bless you all.

The Bible

NOTES

1	John 15:13	41	Isaiah 50:10
2	Ecclesiastes 4:9	42	1 Corinthians 6:19–20
3	Proverbs 27:10	43	Acts 17:26
4	1 Corinthians 13:4–7	44	Leviticus 19:33–34
5	1 Samuel 16:7	45	Galatians 3:27–28
6	Luke 12:6–7	46	Matthew 10:34–36
7	1 Corinthians 6:19	47	Exodus 20:12
8	Psalm 139:13, 15–16	48	Ephesians 6:1–3
9	Psalm 55:22	49	Proverbs 17:17
10	1 Peter 5:7	50	Genesis 1:28
11	Genesis 1:27	51	1 Corinthians 6:19
12	1 Samuel 16:7	52	John 16:24
13	Isaiah 53:2b–3	53	Matthew 26:39
14	Matthew 26:38	54	Isaiah 55:8–9
15	Matthew 28:20	55	James 1:6–8
16	2 Timothy 4:17	56	Proverbs 3:5–6
17	Luke 22:43	57	Psalm 31:9–10
18	John 14:18	58	Romans 8:1
19	John 14:1	59	Isaiah 55:8–9
20	Isaiah 41:10	60	Psalm 27:14
21	Psalm 147:3	61	Psalm 46:1–3
22	John 7:51	62	Psalm 46:7
23	John 19:39	63	Matthew 11:28
24	Matthew 1:22–23	64	Psalm 61:1–2
25	Matthew 2:5–6, quoting Micah 5:2	65	Matthew 11:19
26	Psalm 46:1–3, 7	66	Proverbs 20:1
27	Romans 3:23 (NIV)	67	Proverbs 23:29–35
28	Matthew 26:41	68	Ephesians 5:18
29	Psalm 51:1–4, 7, 10	69	Genesis 14:18–19
30	Genesis 1:27	70	John 2:1–10
31	Psalm 139:13–16	71	1 Timothy 5:23
32	John 10:10	72	Deuteronomy 14:25–26
33	Psalm 51:10, 12	73	Psalm 104:14–15
34	Philippians 4:6	74	Deuteronomy 7:13
35	Psalm 42:11	75	Genesis 1:26
36	Romans 12:2	76	Acts 17:28
37	Matthew 6:33–34	77	Exodus 20:13 (RSV)
38	Philippians 4:13	78	Joshua 14:10
39	Psalm 32:3–7	79	Psalm 66:9
40	Psalm 139:23–24	80	Ecclesiastes 3:1–2

81   Jeremiah 1:4
82   Taken from an article on the Internet
      about Cicely Saunders
83   1 Timothy 6:10
84   Leviticus 25:36–37
85   Matthew 6:25–26
86   Psalm 37:3–4
87   Matthew 6:19–21
88   Matthew 6:24
89   1 Corinthians 10:31—11:1
90   1 Timothy 6:10
91   Genesis 2:15
92   Exodus 20:9
93   2 Thessalonians 3:10
94   Proverbs 6:6–11
95   Matthew 6:31–34
96   1 Timothy 6:6
97   Proverbs 15:27
98   James 4:7–8
99   Job 9:4, 15
100 1 Corinthians 10:13
101 Matthew 6:13
102 Genesis 38:9–10
103 Matthew 5:27–30
104 Psalm 69:30
105 1 Corinthians 6:19–20
106 Romans 15:4
107 Matthew 11:28
108 Psalm 34:18
109 Hebrews 4:16
110 Acts 17:26
111 Mark 12:31
112 Luke 12:22–23, 31
113 Psalm 23:6
114 Proverbs 23:12
115 Colossians 3:23
116 Jeremiah 29:11
117 Ephesians 6:1–4
118 Matthew 6:24–26, 33
119 Proverbs 20:24
120 1 John 5:14–15
121 Exodus 20:14
122 Proverbs 5:6
123 Luke 18:18–20
124 Proverbs 21:21
125 John 8:2–11
126 1 Timothy 1:15
127 Philippians 4:13
128 Psalm 23:1–3
129 Matthew 19:9
130 Psalm 121:1–6
131 Genesis 2:24
132 Hebrews 2:14
133 Matthew 11:28
134 Hebrews 13:5, quoting
      Deuteronomy 31:6, 8
135 1 Peter 5:7
136 Romans 15:4

INDEX OF TOPICS

God's Reality Show

Starring eleven Old Testament housemates

What if—by some strange miracle—eleven key Old Testament characters find themselves having to spend a week together in a tent in the wilderness? Imagine Eve, Noah, Joseph, Moses, Joshua, Rahab, Deborah, Samson, Ruth, Saul and David lifted out of their own time and context into the ultimate reality show, masterminded by the Lord God himself...

Will they manage to get along or will it all be a disaster from start to finish? Will the others gang up on Eve and blame her for bringing sin into the world? Will Saul and David simply end up killing each other? How will Samson conduct himself with the ladies? And what does the Lord God want of them, anyway? Find out what happens by joining author Mike Coles for a special viewing of *God's Reality Show*.

ISBN 1 84101 367 6   £6.99
Available from your local Christian bookshop or, in case of difficulty, direct from BRF using the order form on page 111.

So You Think You're a New Testament Writer

In an exclusive series of interviews, your host Mike Coles brings you five encounters with the men who shaped the New Testament. This is your chance to meet Matthew, Mark, Luke and John, as well as Paul. Discover what motivated them and their writings, and find out more about the consequences of their life-changing encounters with Jesus Christ, known personally to four of them. The live—and lively—studio audience add a whole lot of questions and comment.

Is Paul's anti-women reputation deserved? Can we trust a reformed tax collector to tell the truth? What's the amazing new 'revelation' that John claims to have had on his island of exile? And where can you get hold of the best wine, olive oil, or donkeys, in town? In *So You Think You're a New Testament Writer* you'll find answers to these questions!

ISBN 1 84101 183 5   £6.99
Available from your local Christian bookshop or, in case of difficulty, direct from BRF using the order form on page 111.

The Bible in Cockney

Well, bits of it anyway...

Read how Jesus feeds five thousand geezers with just five loaves of Uncle Fred and two Lilian Gish. Or how Noah built a bloomin' massive nanny. Then there's always the story of David and that massive geezer Goliath, or the time when Simon's finger and thumb-in-law was Tom and Dick in Uncle Ned and Jesus healed her...

ISBN 1 84101 217 3   £5.99

More Bible in Cockney

Prophets, proverbs and pioneers

This book has a butcher's at some of the proverbs and psalms as well as the Ding Dong of Ding Dongs. We'll also find out about some of those great Old Testament prophets who got in a right old two-and-eight 'cos of the way the Israelites worshipped dodgy idols.

To finish off, we have a complete translation of the Captain Hook of Acts into Cockney. Read how Jesus' early followers spread the good news about 'im and find out how Christianity began among the Jewish people, but soon became a faith for the whole world...

ISBN 1 84101 259 9   £6.99
Available from your local Christian bookshop or, in case of difficulty, direct from BRF using the order form on page 111.

ORDER FORM

REF	TITLE	PRICE	QTY	TOTAL
367 6	*God's Reality Show*	£6.99		
183 5	*So You Think You're a New Testament Writer*	£6.99		
217 3	*The Bible in Cockney*	£5.99		
259 9	*More Bible in Cockney*	£6.99		

POSTAGE AND PACKING CHARGES					
order value	UK	Europe	Surface	Air Mail	Postage and packing:
£7.00 & under	£1.25	£3.00	£3.50	£5.50	Donation:
£7.01–£30.00	£2.25	£5.50	£6.50	£10.00	Total enclosed:
Over £30.00	free	prices on request			

Name _____ Account Number _____

Address _____

_____ Postcode _____

Telephone Number _____ Email _____

Payment by: Cheque ❑ Mastercard ❑ Visa ❑ Postal Order ❑ Switch ❑

Credit card no. ❑❑❑❑ ❑❑❑❑ ❑❑❑❑ ❑❑❑❑ Expires ❑❑ ❑❑

Switch card no. ❑❑❑❑❑❑❑❑❑❑❑❑❑❑❑❑❑❑

Issue no. of Switch card ❑❑❑❑ Expires ❑❑ ❑❑

Signature _____ Date _____

All orders must be accompanied by the appropriate payment.

Please send your completed order form to:
BRF, First Floor, Elsfield Hall, 15–17 Elsfield Way, Oxford OX2 8FG
Tel. 01865 319700 / Fax. 01865 319701 Email: enquiries@brf.org.uk

❑ Please send me further information about BRF publications.

Available from your local Christian bookshop.   **BRF is a Registered Charity**

brf

Resourcing your spiritual journey

through...

- Bible reading notes
- Books for Advent & Lent
- Books for Bible study and prayer
- Books to resource those working with
  under 11s in school, church and at home

- Quiet days and retreats
- Training for primary teachers
  and children's leaders
- Godly Play
- Barnabas Live

For more information, visit the **brf** website at **www.brf.org.uk**